OLD TESTAMENT GUIDES

General Editor
R.N. Whybray

ZEPHANIAH, HABAKKUK, JOEL

ZEPHANIAH
HABAKKUK
JOEL

Rex Mason

Published by JSOT Press
for the Society for Old Testament Study

Copyright © 1994 Sheffield Academic Press

Published by JSOT Press
JSOT Press is an imprint of
Sheffield Academic Press Ltd
343 Fulwood Road
Sheffield S10 3BP
England

Typeset by Sheffield Academic Press
and
Printed on acid-free paper in Great Britain
by Charlesworth Group
Huddersfield

British Library Cataloguing in Publication Data

Mason, Rex
    Zephaniah, Habakkuk, Joel.—(Old
    Testament Guides, ISSN 0264-6498)
    I. Title II. Series
    224

ISBN 1-85075-718-6

CONTENTS

ACKNOWLEDGMENTS

I am most grateful to Professor Whybray as General Editor of the Old Testament Guides series and to Ms Helen Tookey, the Desk Editor at JSOT Press involved with the production of this book, for their expert and careful help in the early and later stages of its preparation. Blemishes and shortcomings which remain are my responsibility but would have been far more numerous without their guidance.

ABBREVIATIONS

ASTI	*Annual of the Swedish Theological Institute*
ATD	Das Alte Testament Deutsch
AV	Authorized Version
BA	*Biblical Archaeologist*
Bib	*Biblica*
BJRL	*Bulletin of the John Rylands University Library of Manchester*
BKAT	Biblischer Kommentar: Altes Testament
BWANT	Beiträge zur Wissenschaft vom Alten und Neuen Testament
BZ	*Biblische Zeitschrift*
BZAW	Beihefte zur *ZAW*
CAT	Commentaire de l'Ancien Testament
CB	Century Bible
CBC	Cambridge Bible Commentary on the New English Bible
CBQ	*Catholic Biblical Quarterly*
CBS	The Cambridge Bible for Schools
EvT	*Evangelische Theologie*
ExpTim	*Expository Times*
HAT	Handbuch zum Alten Testament
HTR	*Harvard Theological Review*
HUCA	*Hebrew Union College Annual*
IB	*Interpreter's Bible*
ICC	International Critical Commentary
ITC	International Theological Commentary
JBL	*Journal of Biblical Literature*
JNES	*Journal of Near Eastern Studies*
JSOT	*Journal for the Study of the Old Testament*
JSOTSup	*Journal for the Study of the Old Testament* Supplement Series
JTS	*Journal of Theological Studies*
KAT	Kommentar zum Alten Testament
NCB	New Century Bible
NEB	*New English Bible*
NICOT	New International Commentary on the Old Testament

OBO	Orbis biblicus et orientalis
OTG	Old Testament Guides
OTL	Old Testament Library
PCB	*Peake's Commentary on the Bible*
RSR	*Recherches de science religieuse*
RSV	Revised Standard Version
SB	Sources bibliques
SBLDS	Society of Biblical Literature Dissertation Series
SBT	Studies in Biblical Theology
TBC	Torch Bible Commentaries
TSK	*Theologische Studien und Kritiken*
TOTC	Tyndale Old Testament Commentaries
VT	*Vetus Testamentum*
VTSup	Supplements to *Vetus Testamentum*
WBC	Word Biblical Commentary
WC	Westminster Commentaries
WMANT	Wissenschaftliche Monographien zum Alten und Neuen Testament
ZAW	*Zeitschrift für die alttestamentliche Wissenschaft*
ZB	Zürcher Bibelkommentare
ZDMG	*Zeitschrift der deutschen morganländischen Gesellschaft*

Select List of Commentaries

L.C. Allen, *The Books of Joel, Obadiah, Jonah and Micah* (NICOT; Grand Rapids: Eerdmans, 1976). Offers a very valuable survey of earlier scholarship.

D.W. Baker, *Nahum, Habakkuk and Zephaniah* (TOTC; London: Tyndale Press, 1988). Written from a theologically conservative point of view but with due acknowledgment of previous scholarly work.

L.H. Brockington, 'Joel', *PCB*, pp. 614-16. Somewhat dated, in a volume shortly to be revised.

J.H. Eaton, *Obadiah, Nahum, Habakkuk, Zephaniah* (TBC; London: SCM Press, 1961). An excellent introduction which gives full weight to the cultic elements in the books.

J.P. Hyatt, 'Habakkuk', 'Zephaniah', *PCB*, pp. 637-42. A brief and simple introduction to the two books by a scholar who specialized in their study over many years.

D.R. Jones, *Isaiah 56–66 and Joel* (TBC; Philadelphia: Fortress Press, 1964). A brief but useful introduction for the beginner.

G.S. Ogden (with R.R. Deutsch), *Joel and Malachi: A Promise of Hope: A Call to Obedience* (ITC; Grand Rapids: Eerdmans, 1987). This series is somewhat conservative in its stance but a great deal of information is packed into a small space and represents much original investigation.

J.J.M. Roberts, *Nahum, Habakkuk and Zephaniah* (OTL; Louisville, KY: Westminster Press/John Knox, 1991). Unfortunately this book was not available to me when I wrote this Guide and has still not been published in the UK. It is a good, standard, 'middle-of-the-road' commentary.

O.P. Robertson, *The Books of Nahum, Habakkuk and Zephaniah* (NICOT; Grand Rapids: Eerdmans, 1990). A useful commentary which suffers from the lack of a full and separate introduction to each book.

J.M.P. Smith (with W.H. Ward and J.A. Bewer), *Zephaniah, Micah, Zechariah, Nahum, Habakkuk, Obadiah, Joel* (ICC; Edinburgh: T. & T. Clark, 1911). This series is now dated but is unsurpassed in its attention to the Hebrew text and the history of early scholarship. Of the three, Smith on Zephaniah is the strongest.

R.L. Smith, *Micah–Malachi* (WBC; Waco, TX: Word Books, 1984). A full and detailed commentary on Habakkuk and Zephaniah which offers an excellent survey of previous scholarship.

D. Stuart, *Hosea–Jonah* (WBC; Waco, TX: Word Books, 1987). The coverage of Joel is adequate but somewhat selective in its attention to earlier scholarship.

C.L. Taylor, 'Habakkuk', 'Zephaniah', *IB*, VI (1952), pp. 973-1036. Taylor's work is a supreme example of the kind of 'literary-critical scholarship' which wields a vigorous axe to cut out 'inauthentic' additions to the words of the prophets.

J.A. Thompson, 'Joel', *IB*, VI, pp. 729-62. An excellent commentary by one who studied the book in great depth over a long period.

H.W. Wolff, *Joel and Amos* (Hermeneia; Philadelphia: Fortress Press, 1977). A powerful argument for the unity of the book of Joel.

Foreign-language commentaries

C.A. Keller, *Osée, Joel, Abdias, Jonas, Amos* (CAT, 11a; Paris: Cerf, 1965).

—*Michée, Nahoum, Habakuk, Sophonie* (CAT, 11b; Paris: Cerf, 2nd edn, 1990).

B. Renaud, *Michée, Sophonie, Nahum* (SB: Paris: Cerf, 1987).

W. Rudolph, *Joel, Amos, Obadja, Jona* (KAT, 13.2; Gütersloh: Gerd Mohn, 1971).

K. Seybold, *Nahum, Habakuk, Zephanja* (ZB; Zürich: Theologischer Verlag, 1991).

A. Weiser, *Das Buch der zwölf kleinen Propheten* (ATD, 24.1; Göttingen: Vandenhoeck & Ruprecht, 1967).

1
INTRODUCTION

A LONG FAMILIAR STORY tells of the man who was given a dictionary by a friend as a birthday present. When, later, the friend met him and asked how he was enjoying it he replied, 'It is all very well, but I seem to lose the thread of the story so quickly'.

Those who come for the first time to the study of the Old Testament prophetic books may well feel some sympathy for him. There seems, at first glance at least, and often after many glances, to be little apparent order in the way the contents are arranged. It is difficult to follow any logical development of argument or shape to the presentation of ideas. Often what look like quite contradictory concepts appear within a short space of each other. What are we to make of it all?

When we visit an ancient church we can usually see traces of its use by a worshipping community who lived and prayed there through many centuries in widely varying circumstances. Here is a Norman arch, there a perpendicular nave. Here are signs of Victorian restoration and enlargement (regarded as much more respectable now than it was earlier in this century!) and perhaps there is also a modern addition. That is how scholars see the prophetic books. Each, of course, bears evidence of the word of the 'original' prophet, but each also shows signs of reinterpretation and reapplication of that message in changed historical situations as the book has been handed down in a worshipping community of faith. The trouble is that the signs of such a community's literary activity are not always as clear and as easily identifiable as their building work. Stones sometimes cry out more loudly and clearly than words. Nevertheless, this means that the study of the findings of scholars who have examined the books of Zephaniah, Habakkuk and Joel (and the others, but these are the subject of this book—examined in what I believe to be their chronological sequence rather than in their canonical order) is no mere arid intellectual and academic exercise. It is work which enables us to see and hear something of the people of faith across many years who found inspiration in the message of a particular prophet and sought, in a living and creative way, to apply that message to the signs and events of their own changing times and circumstances.

Part I

ZEPHANIAH

2

THE PROPHETIC CORPUS
IN MINIATURE

THE BOOK OF ZEPHANIAH contains only three chapters; yet
these encompass many of the features that we find in the
prophetic books as a whole. We hear echoes of prophets like
Amos, Micah and Isaiah in their indictments of Israel for the
injustice and oppression of its ruling classes, although, as with
Hosea and Ezekiel, there is greater emphasis on Israel's sins
of religious apostasy and unfaithfulness. Such indictments are
followed by the threat of God's judgment on his own people in
the form of invasion and battle, associated especially with 'the
Day of the Lord', which is, again, described in terms reminiscent especially of Amos and Isaiah. As with some other
prophets there is a call for repentance in the hope that such
judgment might be averted. As in all the major prophetic
books there is a group of oracles threatening divine judgment
against foreign nations. Equally, as in most of the other prophetic books, there are hopes held out of salvation for Israel in
a time when God will intervene on their behalf. He will
avenge Israel against their enemies and again rule as king in
his holy city, Jerusalem, defending it against all comers. He
will bring back those of its citizens who have been taken away
as captives to foreign lands and establish a rule of justice which
will make for righteousness among his own people. Some
easing of the logical tension between the threats of total judgment and these hopes of a glorious future is found here, as in
some other prophets—notably Isaiah—in a doctrine of an
Israelite 'remnant', that band of people whom God will preserve
through the crisis and purify so that they may fulfil his ideals

for his people as a humble, trusting and righteous community.

All this is seen as the action of God in history. Indeed, some signs of that activity are already apparent; and the others, it seems, will follow in the immediate future. But there are also suggestions in the book of a wider, almost 'trans-historical' view of God's action in the future. In places, his actions against his own people are extended to a worldwide—one may almost say 'cosmic'—dimension which can only be described as a reversal of his work of creation, a plunging of it back into the primeval chaos which existed before he imposed order on it in the way described in Genesis 1. Likewise, the picture of future salvation seems to be extended to include all the nations and the restoration to the earth of almost paradisiacal conditions. So some have found in this book traces of the 'apocalyptic' elements which occur elsewhere in the prophetic corpus: that is, a belief that God will break into this world's history from outside and beyond it, to set up a quite new age in which the world will return to its former condition when God first created it 'good', or a 'Paradise'—a belief frequently distinguished by scholars from the prophetic view of God's action in which he is seen to be working through the events of this world's history to achieve new conditions in the present age.

In all these ways, then, Zephaniah encapsulates in miniature almost the whole range of Old Testament prophecy. These ideas are also expressed in literary forms similar to those employed by the other prophets. Most of the book is in poetry, and it utilizes many of the poetic devices the prophets loved to employ, such as wordplay, assonance, vivid simile and metaphor. It uses the familiar 'messenger' formulae, such as 'says the LORD', or 'says the LORD of hosts', although strangely, not the most familiar of them all, 'Thus says the LORD'. It alternates, as do the other prophets, between expressing its message as direct, first-person speech of Yahweh and third-person reported speech of the prophet.

Above all, it is not made any clearer here than in the other Old Testament prophetic books how, at one and the same time, God can judge the nations, avenging the wrongs they have done to his people, and yet promise that foreigners will also join his own people in sharing in the fruits of his reign as universal king. We are faced with the same intractable problem of deciding how all the many elements which make up such a prophetic book as this actually came together. Can they all be the work of one writer and the product of the same historical context? If not, how can we tell which were the words of the original prophet (whoever exactly that may have been) and what has been added to them? And, if we can detect 'layers' in the book, can we identify them and decide with what purposes they were added? And, when we have attempted all that, what is there left to say about the value and the purpose of the final form of the book as it has come down to us?

3

THE CONTENTS OF THE
BOOK OF ZEPHANIAH

1.1: Superscription

THIS GIVES A GENEALOGY of Zephaniah, unique in its length
for a prophet, and sets the time of his prophetic activity in the
reign of Josiah, King of Judah (640–609 BCE).

1.2-18: The Day of Yahweh's Judgment
on Judah and Jerusalem

Judah is indicted for syncretistic worship, the people having
replaced worship of Yahweh with worship of other deities (1.4-
5). Some have abandoned the worship of Yahweh altogether
(1.6). Some prominent members of the community and court
circles have adopted foreign ways of life and have been guilty
of amassing wealth by force and deceit (1.8-9). This has been
accompanied by oppression of the poor (1.9. See Keller,
Gerleman, Eaton and Sabottka for discussion of the exact
meaning of the charge of v. 9a). Not unnaturally these people
who prospered were complacent; and they are vividly described as wine thickening on the lees (1.12)—that is, wine
which deteriorates in quality for being left undisturbed (cf.
Jer. 48.11).

Judgment against these people is announced. Yahweh 'will
stretch out his hand' in hostile action against them (1.4). The
'Day of Yahweh' is likened to a sacrifice to which Yahweh
invites his 'guests'. Whoever these may be, there is no doubt
as to the identity of the victim. Fittingly, the summons to the
'sacrifice' takes the form of a cultic call to prepare for Yahweh's

theophany: 'Be silent' (cf. Hab. 2.20; Zech. 2.13 [Heb. 2.17]).
No quarter of the holy city will be spared 'on that day' (1.10-
11), while in 1.12 Yahweh is pictured as seeking out the evil-
doers in Jerusalem with lamps. The complacent, idolatrous
rich will know the kind of despoiling of their goods that they
have handed out to others (1.13)—a judgment reinforced by a
threat also found in Amos 5.11.

Most of the indictment and announcement of judgment is
expressed in first-person divine speech. This breaks down in
v. 6 (which a number of commentators find to be secondary
for this reason and also because of its 'Deuteronomistic'
language) and, not surprisingly, in v. 7, which appears to be a
form of cultic summons familiar from temple worship, while 8a
links this to the divine speech which resumes thereafter. Verses
14-18, in third-person speech, appear to be a kind of hymn
describing the terrors of 'the Day of Yahweh' in terms
reminiscent of earlier prophets (for example Amos 5.18-20,
Isa. 2.12-22).

This section, one of judgment against Judah and Jerusalem,
is set in a framework (vv. 2-3, 17-18) which describes the
judgment as not only directed against God's own people but as
universal, even cosmic, in scope. 1.2-3 threatens the revoca-
tion of God's original act of creation when he brought order
out of chaos (Gen. 1). All the elements of creation described
there appear here in reverse order to those described in Gen. 1
(see de Roche).

In treating 1.2-18 as a unit I am not at the moment making
any judgment about its original, or present, unity. Such issues
remain to be discussed in Chapter 7.

2.1-3: A Call to Penitence

There are difficulties of translation in v. 1 which, together
with the lack of precise details, make it unclear who is being
addressed. Indeed, J.M.P. Smith links this verse with the
oracle against the Philistines which follows. Such a view
would be easier to hold if it were assumed that v. 3 is wholly
or partly a later addition, as several scholars have taken it to
be (for example Taylor, Elliger, Seybold). However, Hyatt,

Renaud and others have argued for the unity of 2.1-3, and Elliger sees at least 3b as genuine and as addressed to the Judaean community. At the least we must say that v. 3, either originally or by way of early commentary on the passage, implies that these verses are addressed to the people of Judah; for only they, or some of them, could be addressed as the 'humble' or 'poor' of the land who would be 'hidden' on the day of Yahweh's wrath—an idea clearly akin to Isaiah's words to the people in Isa. 2.10, 19, 21.

The passage as a whole is a call to repent. Logically such a call seems strange after the threat of apparently total judgment in ch. 1, but there is a similar sequence in Amos (5.4-5). The 'perhaps' of v. 3 may suggest that hope lies in the mercy of God alone.

2.4-15: Oracles against Foreign Nations

In this section oracles of judgment are directed against the Philistine cities (vv. 4-7), Moab and Ammon (vv. 8-11), Egypt (v. 12) and Assyria (vv. 13-15). These represent Israel's enemies to the west, east, south and north; they appear to have been chosen as typical examples, symbolizing the threats faced by Israel from all quarters at different times in their history. God's decisive action against them also serves to illustrate his *universal* power over all parts of the earth (cf. Fohrer). I am indebted to Dr Stephanie Dalley for drawing my attention to the fact that in Mesopotamia kings only earned certain titles such as 'Lord of the Four Quarters of the Earth' after they had conducted a number of successful military campaigns (see Liverain); this would strengthen the notion here of Yahweh's universal kingship. Renaud makes the point that similar geographical schemes are found in the oracles against the nations in Amos, Ezekiel 25 and Jeremiah 46–49. This tendency to see certain enemies as 'typical' suggests that caution is necessary when we try to determine specific historical contexts for each oracle and so, by such means, to date Zephaniah. We cannot know for certain what references he had in mind or how any original oracles of his may have been understood and interpreted in the course of the book's development.

The passage is characterized by play on the names of the cities and the fates reserved for them, certainly in the cases of Gaza, Ashdod and Ekron and perhaps also of Ashkelon (see Thomas). Further, the name 'Cretan' is echoed in v. 6 in a probably deliberate use of a rare word usually translated 'pasture' or 'meadow'. Many commentators believe that v. 7 is a later addition since it appears to contradict the totality of the destruction predicted in vv. 4-6 and perhaps suggests much later, post-exilic hopes.

Moab and Ammon are censured for their 'taunts' and 'boasts' (a traditional expression of human hubris and defiance of God; cf. Isa. 10.12-19; Ezek. 28.2-10) and possibly for the enlargement of their territory at the expense of Israel. The idea of their own territory's being taken over by the survivors of Judah appears here (v. 9), so if v. 7 is secondary, this verse must be also. The limitation of this repossession to only a 'remnant' of Judah may be an editor's attempt to reconcile this passage with 1.2–2.3. It shows in any event how such oracles could be applied later in terms of promise to those who had survived the Babylonian exile. Some scholars take vv. 10 and 11 as additional, some only v. 11 (both verses are prose whereas what has preceded and what follows is poetry). These verses serve to make these peoples typical examples of pride and defiance against Yahweh and so help us to see how oracles which may once have had a specific setting could be later given a much wider and more general application (see Cresson for examples of how this happened with Edom after the exile).

The final oracle against Assyria is an ironic attack on its moral attitude of self-confidence and self-reliance (cf. Isa. 10.5-19). If this oracle is in fact a prediction of a future event it must be dated to before the fall of Nineveh, to an alliance of Medes and Babylonians in 612 BCE. However, those who date Zephaniah later than that (for example Hyatt) speak of this as 'prophecy after the event'. Again, however, the oracle may be seen as a typical embodiment of the kind of moral attitudes which are sure to bring about Yahweh's judgment.

The function of judgment oracles against foreign nations seems to be to act as 'salvation oracles' for Israel (see Westermann). However, we must not forget that such oracles could also be employed as indictments of Israel, as in Amos (cf. Barton). Possibly here also the placing of an accusation against Judah and Jerusalem immediately afterwards and the mention of Yahweh's actions against the nations as a warning to his own people (3.6-7) suggests that, at least in the present form of the book, they are meant to have a function similar to that of the foreign oracles in the book of Amos. Perhaps the examples they offer of Yahweh's judgments against certain moral attitudes and actions in general, rather than simply of his action against particular nations, were meant to serve as a warning to later generations of Judaeans after the exile not to show similar attitudes themselves.

3.1-8: Further Indictments against the
Jerusalem Community

Again those addressed are not specified, but vv. 3-5 make it clear that the reference must be the Jerusalem community, although Renaud, who links vv. 1-8 under the single heading 'Jerusalem and the Nations', wonders if the ambiguity is deliberate (especially in the light of 2.15), aiming to put the punishment of Jerusalem and the nations into the same context.

The attack on the community as a whole concerns their general disobedience towards God; indeed, so general and imprecise are the charges of vv. 1-5 that C.L. Taylor doubts whether the passage is original. The charges against particular groups of leaders—officials, judges, prophets and priests—echo those of most of the pre-exilic prophets. The contrast with Yahweh himself who is 'within' the city (as they were accustomed to claim in their worship; see for example Ps. 46.5) to give true judgments in the mornings (the time when the king heard appeals; cf. Jer. 21.12) is a deliberate, ironic accusation. Eaton wonders if v. 5 is a quotation from a temple hymn. If so, its irony would be even more pointed.

Verses 6-7 seem to suggest that Yahweh's actions against

the unrighteous nations should have offered a warning to Israel. Since the form of the prophecy changes in v. 6 to first-person divine speech, some have seen a new section beginning here. Keller, for example, sees vv. 6-13 as a unit to which he gives the heading 'Yahweh's Political Action', and Elliger also sees vv. 6-8 as a new unit. J.M.P. Smith describes vv. 6-7 as two separate intrusions having nothing to do with each other or with their present context, while Taylor sees them as an addition, expanding the thought of v. 2 that Jerusalem remained obdurate to all Yahweh's attempts at discipline.

In any event, the relation of vv. 1-7 and 9-13 to v. 8 remains a most difficult problem. As it stands v. 8 speaks of Yahweh's judgment against the nations; but this is totally unexpected. After the indictment of Jerusalem we expect some announcement of judgment, and the word 'therefore' usually introduces this. R.L. Smith looks for a way out by suggesting that those addressed here may be 'the pious remnant in Judah'; but this does not really avoid the problem. Renaud, who reads vv. 1-8 as a unit, suggests that originally the text may have read 'to pour out upon *you* my indignation' and thus have spoken originally of Yahweh's intention to gather the nations to use them against Jerusalem in judgment. This, he supposed, was subsequently changed by the same editor whose hand is also seen in 1.2-3 and 17-18 who wanted to show Yahweh's action against Judah to be a universal one—a view shared by Elliger.

3.9-13: Salvation for Judah and the Nations

The section opens with an extraordinary change of fate for the nations when contrasted with the present form of v. 8. This passage predicts no less than their conversion to the worship of Yahweh. J.M.P. Smith thought of it as a later addition designed to soften the impact of v. 8, while vv. 11-13 formed the conclusion to the original oracle against Judah. It is now, however, a promise addressed to the faithful among that community. Renaud saw Yahweh's actions described in vv. 8 and 9 as simultaneous, illustrative of both the negative and positive aspects of the Day of Yahweh. Elliger believed that vv. 9-10 were addressed originally to Yahweh's own people but were later changed to include the nations. The picture of the restoration of the community in vv. 12-13 shows at every point the exact reversal of their previous condition described in 1.4-13 and 3.1-4.

3.14-20: Yahweh's Reign as King in Jerusalem

A glorious future is foretold in which Yahweh's reign as universal king in Jerusalem, judging and defeating his people's enemies, is described. The community is called upon to celebrate this prediction in worship, perhaps in anticipation. Many commentators have found parallels here with the so-called 'Enthronement Psalms' which celebrate Yahweh's rule in Jerusalem as king of the world (for example Pss. 47, 93, 96, 97, 98, 99). If the passage is of cultic origin, this might account for the fact that it concentrates on the military defeat of the community's enemies and the reputation of God's people among the nations rather than on their rescue from the kinds of sins described earlier in the book. The great majority of commentators see at least v. 20 as a later, post-exilic addition promising the return of Israelites who had been deported at the time of the Babylonian exile. Thus the book would end with a superb note of encouragement to later generations, themselves no doubt living in difficult and challenging circumstances, to heed the warnings of the earlier prophet and be sustained by the hopes the writer entertained in consequence of his faith in the sovereignty of Yahweh.

Further Reading

J. Barton, *Amos's Oracles against the Nations* (Cambridge: Cambridge University Press, 1980).

B.C. Cresson, 'The Condemnation of Edom in Post-Exilic Judaism', in J.F. Efird (ed.), *The Use of the Old Testament in the New and Other Essays* (Durham, NC: Duke University Press, 1972), pp. 125-48.

Eaton, *Obadiah, Nahum, Habakkuk, Zephaniah.*

K. Elliger, *Das Buch der zwölf Kleinen Propheten. II. Die propheten Nahum, Habakuk, Zephanja, Haggai, Sacharja, Maleachi* (ATD, 25; Göttingen: Vandenhoeck & Ruprecht, 1964).

G. Fohrer, 'Prophetie und Magie', *ZAW* 78 (1966), pp. 25-47.

G. Gerleman, *Zephanja textkritisch und literarisch Untersucht* (Lund: Gleerup, 1942).

J.P. Hyatt, 'The Date and Background of Zephaniah', *JNES* 7 (1948), pp. 25-29.

—'Zephaniah', pp. 640-42.

Keller, *Michée, Nahoum, Habakuk, Sophonie.*

M. Liverain, 'Critique of Variants and the Titulary of Sennacherib', in F.M. Fales (ed.), *Assyrian Royal Inscriptions: New Horizons* (Rome: Istituto per l'Oriente, 1981).

Renaud, *Michée, Sophonie, Nahum.*

M. de Roche, 'Zephaniah 1:2, 3: The Sweeping of Creation'; 'Contra Creation, Covenant & Conquest', *VT* 30 (1980), pp. 104-109, 280-90.

L. Sabottka, *Zephanja: Versuch einer Neuübersetzung mit philologischen Kommentar* (Rome: Pontifical Biblical Institute, 1972).

K. Seybold, 'Die Verwendung der Bildmotive in der Prophetie Zefanjas', in H. Weippert *et al.* (eds.), *Beiträge zur prophetischen Bildsprache in Israel und Assyrien* (OBO, 64; Göttingen: Vandenhoeck & Ruprecht, 1985), pp. 30-54.

J.M.P. Smith, *Zephaniah, Micah, Zechariah, Nahum, Habakkuk, Obadiah, Joel*, pp. 159-81.

R.L. Smith, *Micah–Malachi.*

Taylor, 'Zephaniah', pp. 1007-36.

D.W. Thomas, 'A Pun on the Name of Ashdod in Zeph. 2.4', *ExpTim* 74 (1962–63), p. 63.

C. Westermann, *Basic Forms of Prophetic Speech* (London: Lutterworth, 1967).

4
ZEPHANIAH
THE PROPHET

THE OPENING VERSE of the book may encourage the reader to feel that a lot can be known about Zephaniah the man. He is given a genealogy stretching back four generations, and this is unique for a prophet. Indeed, only one other example of such a genealogy occurs in the whole of the Old Testament (Jer. 36.14). That is of some slight interest since it refers to one 'Jehudi' who has an ancestor named Cushi, the same name as Zephaniah's father. 'Cushi' could be a personal name, but it also means 'Ethiopian', and this at least raises the question whether an editor thought that someone who may have come from foreign, perhaps immigrant stock needed a longer pedigree to justify his true 'Jewishness' (see for example ben Zvi). The most striking thing about Zephaniah's ancestry, however, is that it is traced back to Hezekiah; and this has given rise to speculation as to whether this was King Hezekiah of Judah (715–687 BCE). Opinions tend to be divided between those who argue that if the king of that name was meant he would have been called 'king of Judah' and those who say that the name of the king was so well known that it needed no such explanation. Questions of chronology have also been discussed. Josiah was a third-generation descendant of King Hezekiah, so could Zephaniah and Josiah have been contemporaries as the superscription says? This is, of course, possible; but the difficulty is one reason which has led some scholars to suggest that the superscription is wrong in setting Zephaniah's ministry in the reign of Josiah, and that his activity should be placed, rather, in the reign of Jehoiakim (see below). The result of all this seems to be that the superscription leaves us in the dark about the prophet's background.

Nor does his name help us. It probably means something like 'Yahweh hides' or 'protects' although some (for example J.M.P. Smith, Watts and Sabottka) have suggested that the name means 'Yahweh is Zaphon', Zaphon being the name of a Canaanite deity who gave his name to 'Mount Zaphon' which is described in the religious literature as the abode of the gods. But the name tells us nothing about the prophet, and it was apparently fairly common in ancient Israel. Four people are so named in the Old Testament (see 2 Kgs 25.18/Jer. 52.24-27 and Jer. 21.1; 37.3; 1 Chron. 6.36; Zech. 6.10, 14 for the others). The suggestion of D.L. Williams that the prophet is to be equated with a priest who was taken by the Babylonians and killed at the time of Zedekiah's rebellion (2 Kgs 25.18-21/Jer. 52.24-27) is without foundation and improbable. What Williams says of the prophet's cultic knowledge is correct; but this is insufficient evidence on which to base an identification with a particular priest of that name of whom we happen by chance to have some knowledge.

All kinds of inferences about the man Zephaniah have been made from his book. It seems safe to deduce that he knew Jerusalem well and looked at things from the perspective of one of its citizens (cf. 1.10-12; 3.1-5). Less secure is the argument that, as one who had royal blood in his veins, he avoided criticizing the king himself while attacking other court and cultic officials (see for example 1.8-9). There could be other reasons for this if, for example, King Josiah was still a minor or had shown himself enthusiastic for religious and political reform. Zephaniah shows such great sympathy and concern for the 'little people' of society (cf. 1.9; 2.3; 3.5, 12-13) that it is difficult to imagine him as belonging to the royal family.

There are a number of sayings recorded in the book which show familiarity with Israel's cultic worship. The prophet finds it natural to liken Yahweh's judgment of his people to a sacrifice for which the invited guests are sanctified and to which they are summoned by the cultic cry 'Be silent' (cf. Hab. 2.20, Zech. 2.13 [Heb. 2.17]). The verb he uses for the 'sweeping away' of creation in 1.2-3 is related to the Hebrew word for the feast of 'Asiph', the 'Ingathering' of the vintage and fruit harvest or the 'Feast of Tabernacles'. He refers to the dispensing of justice by Yahweh 'in the morning', presumably effected through king and cultic officials who pronounced on innocence and guilt (3.5; see Ziegler). He issues a call to worship with the summons to 'seek' Yahweh (2.3), while in 1.6, where the people are charged with failing to do this, the same verb 'to seek' is used in parallel with a quite technical cultic word 'to enquire' of Yahweh. There is an echo of the cultic claims of Yahweh's presence 'in' Jerusalem (3.5; cf. Ps. 46.5). Whether or not 3.14-20 comes from Zephaniah himself, it contains a clear allusion to the language and hopes of Yahweh's universal reign associated with the 'Enthronement Psalms'. Many have believed these psalms to have been the liturgy of an autumnal 'Enthronement Festival' in pre-exilic Jerusalem (see Mowinckel). The very phrase 'Day of Yahweh' is believed by many to be of cultic origin, referring to the theophany of Yahweh at the high point of the people's worship (cf. Pss. 50.1-6; 96.10-13, and see Keller and Renaud). Other scholars trace its origin to the concept of Yahweh's going out at the head of the Israelite army, or with his heavenly host on the day of battle, or they relate it to some traditional hope for an unspecified intervention of God in the future (see Černý and Weiss. The issue is discussed in all the commentaries). The point has already been made that Zephaniah, like Hosea and Ezekiel (the latter being the son of a priest if not a priest himself; the Hebrew of Ezek. 1.3 is ambiguous) attacked mainly the sins of religious apostasy, syncretism and cultic malpractice. Keller and others have pointed out that the word 'place' (*māqôm*) used in 1.4, where God says, 'I will cut off from *this* place the remnant of Baal', is often used in the restricted sense of 'temple'.

It has become a commonplace in Old Testament scholarship that alongside the priests in the sanctuary of Jerusalem 'cultic prophets' were also functioning (see Haldar, Johnson, Mowinckel, Eaton). The task of these was both to present the prayers of the worshipping community to God and to bring God's word to the congregation. Both these functions are seen in some of the Psalms where a human speaker is clearly interceding on behalf of the community, but where there are also 'oracular' sections in which God speaks either in the first person or through the lips of the psalmist (for example Pss. 60, 81, 95). The cultic allusions in the book of Zephaniah have led some scholars to suggest that he was one of these cult prophets. The cultic argument has in fact rested on a broader base than this. Many have found it difficult to see how all the elements of accusation, threat of apparently total judgment, call to repentance, promises of salvation, threats against the 'nations' and promise that the nations will ultimately worship Yahweh all fit logically together. It is the tension between these elements which has led many scholars to question the unity of the book; but some have argued differently, saying that the book mirrors and expresses all the elements that were present together in Israel's cultic worship, especially in the autumnal festival of Yahweh's enthronement at the beginning of the new agricultural year. This is the argument of Eaton, who says, 'It is not impossible that Zephaniah designed his work for recitation in the course of the temple services', and 'it is in any case probable that the liturgical practice of Zephaniah's time has decisively influenced the arrangement, ideas and language of the composition'. Watts shows sympathy for this view.

One further point should be noted. By whatever means, Zephaniah appears to have been familiar with the ideas of earlier prophets, especially Amos and Isaiah. He echoes what those two prophets have to say about the Day of Yahweh as a day of darkness and judgment for their people (Zeph. 1.14-18; 3.8; cf. Amos 5.18-20; Isa. 2.12-19). He shares with Amos a belief in the apparently total nature and irrevocability of God's coming judgment, yet issues an (apparently illogical) call for repentance (Zeph. 2.3; cf. Amos 5.6-7, 14-15). He appears as a champion for the 'poor' and 'humble', terms which appear a great deal in Israel's psalmody but also in Amos and Isaiah, prophets who were both passionately concerned for these people (see Amos 2.6-7; 4.1; Isa. 3.14-15; 10.1-2). There is in Zephaniah an almost 'Isaianic' mistrust of all human self-confidence and arrogance (for example 1.18; 2.15; 3.11; cf.

Isa. 2.12-17; 10.12-16; 30.15). There is also a place given to
the idea of a 'remnant' (Zeph. 2.7; 3.12; cf. Isa. 7.3; 10.20-23).
In both Isaiah and Zephaniah some doubt inevitably arises
concerning the date of such references, but it is wholly
possible that ideas original to the prophet were reapplied in
later circumstances. (For such an idea in relation to the book
of Micah see Mason, and for the idea of the 'remnant' in
Zephaniah see Anderson.) We do not know how the teachings
of the earlier prophets were promulgated before the exile nor
how wide an audience or readership they would have
reached. But familiarity with prophetic ideas suggests something about the circles in which Zephaniah must have moved.

However, even with all these features of his book, we must
be cautious before we label Zephaniah as himself a 'cult' or
'temple' prophet. Despite Eaton and others, it is not obvious
that the present shape of the book follows any clear liturgical
pattern (see the discussion below on Joel). Many of the 'cultic'
allusions are ironic; and it is difficult to believe that a person
who was a paid servant of the temple could have stood quite
so objectively distant from it all and have been so critical of
the worship conducted there. On the other hand, the point
made by Eaton that many of the apparently inconsistent
elements in the book might have been familiar elements in
the worship of the pre-exilic temple in Jerusalem is a valid
one. Such elements may be reflected in a psalm like Psalm 89,
which seems to be written from a situation of defeat and
humiliation for the Davidic king in Jerusalem (vv. 38-51) who
nevertheless renews his trust in Yahweh by his prayer and
takes hope for the future from God's past promises and actions
(vv. 1-37). Similarly the so-called 'Enthronement Psalms' celebrate Yahweh's kingship; but in each there is the suggestion
of a renewal of that kingship in the face of conflict (Pss. 47,
92, 93, 95, 97, 98); and in several of them there is a call for
renewed trust in him and obedience to him. Whether such
psalms reflect a cultic battle or have some basis in historical
events does not affect the point here (for a balanced recent
discussion of these issues see Day). But such considerations
should make us cautious before we say that they cannot all
have been components in the original preaching of the

prophet and so must have been introduced by later editors, each with his own particular axe to grind.

A number of commentators have pointed to another significant case of affinity with the book of Zephaniah, namely Deuteronomy. Recently, D. Palmer Robertson has particularly stressed this. He gives detailed examples of similarity of vocabulary and phraseology between the two books (e.g. 1.13, cf. Deut. 28.30, 39; 1.15, cf. Deut. 28.53, 55, 57, 4.11; 1.17, cf. Deut. 28.29; 1.18, cf. Deut. 32.21-22; 3.17, cf. Deut. 28.63, 30.9; 3.19-20, cf. Deut. 26.19). In addition, Zephaniah shares Deuteronomy's horror of all signs of religious apostasy and of the dilution of the 'pure' worship of the 'pure' people of Yahweh with foreign influences. There is also a link between the two books in their treatment of disobedience to God and judgment on the land.

We must not, however, make too much of all this. We have to be wary of those commentators who see every occurrence of 'Deuteronomic' language as a sign of a later 'Deuteronomistic' editing of a prophetic book. Both books may have been open to similar influences and traditions. Further, there are a number of prominent doctrines in Deuteronomy which are not mentioned by Zephaniah, while many of the parallels of thought are very general and are to be found in most of the pre-exilic prophetic books. What these parallels might suggest, however, is that Zephaniah reflects a general impatience with a diluted form of Yahwism and a desire for reform which are also represented by the Deuteronomists. He, like them, was heavily influenced by the teachings of earlier prophets.

In fact, we do not really know who the 'Deuteronomists' were. Some have thought that they were Levites of the outlying sanctuaries (for example von Rad). Others have maintained that they were prophets (Nicholson). The supposition that there were cult prophets who functioned at the sanctuaries alongside the priests probably makes this debate less relevant. But, whoever they were, they must have commanded support from a sufficiently wide section of the Israelite community for their views to have had the influence that they did. We can say no more about Zephaniah than that he belonged to those who recognized the need for, and worked for, religious reform in obedience to what he and they believed to have been the word of God spoken through the prophets.

However, this lack of knowledge about the biographical details of the prophet need not greatly concern us. It is clear that those who preserved the words and deeds of the prophets were not interested in them as individuals but only in their vital role as those who, they believed, had been called by God to proclaim his word to Israel. Further, it was the continuing relevance of those words and their function in later times which led to their continued use and regard. As R.J. Coggins has pointed out, we are right to be more interested in the final form of the book in our study today than in any alleged ability to be able to give some psychological account of an individual. This view has received powerful endorsement from Ehud ben Zvi (see below). All we can really know about Zephaniah, and all that ultimately matters, is that his preaching and ministry initiated the movement which led finally to the emergence of the book bearing his name and its use in the later tradition.

Further Reading

G.W. Anderson, 'The Idea of the Remnant in the Book of Zephaniah', *ASTI* 11 (1978), pp. 11-14.

E. ben Zvi, *A Historical-Critical Study of the Book of Zephaniah* (BZAW, 198; Giessen: Töpelmann, 1991).

L. Černý, *The Day of Yahweh and Some Relevant Problems* (Prague: University of Karlova, 1948).

R.J. Coggins (with S.P. Re'emi), *Israel among the Nations: A Commentary on the Books of Nahum and Obadiah* (ITC: Grand Rapids: Eerdmans, 1985).

J. Eaton, 'The Psalms and Israelite Worship', in G.W. Anderson (ed.), *Tradition and Interpretation* (Oxford: Clarendon Press, 1979), pp. 238-73.

—*Vision in Worship* (London, 1981).

A. Haldar, *Associations of Cult Prophets among the Ancient Semites* (Uppsala: Almqvist and Wiksell, 1945).

A.R. Johnson, *The Cultic Prophet in Ancient Israel* (Cardiff: University of Wales Press, 2nd edn, 1962).

S. Mowinckel, *The Psalms in Israel's Worship* (trans. D.R. Ap-Thomas; Oxford: Basil Blackwell, 1962).

E.W. Nicholson, *Deuteronomy and Tradition* (Oxford: Basil Blackwell, 1967).

G. von Rad, *Studies in Deuteronomy* (London: SCM Press, 1953).

Robertson, *The Books of Nahum, Habakkuk and Zephaniah*.

J.D. Watts, *The Books of Joel, Obadiah, Jonah, Nahum, Habakkuk and Zephaniah* (CBC; Cambridge: Cambridge University Press, 1975).

M. Weiss, 'The Origin of "The Day of the Lord" Reconsidered', *HUCA* 37 (1966), p. 40.

D.L. Williams, 'The Date of Zephaniah', *JBL* 82 (1963), pp. 77-88.

J. Ziegler, 'Die Hilfe Gottes "am Morgen"', in H. Junker and J. Botterweck (eds.), *Alttestamentliche Studien: Festschrift für F. Nötscher* (Bonn, 1950), pp. 281-88.

5

THE HISTORICAL BACKGROUND

THERE HAS BEEN a great deal of discussion about the precise historical context of Zephaniah's activity. In order to appraise the points at issue it is necessary to sketch briefly the main historical events of the seventh century BCE as they affected Judah; this was a period in which not only Zephaniah and Habakkuk, but perhaps also even Joel, may have been active.

For most of the seventh century the Near East was dominated by the neo-Assyrian empire. Having begun its expansionist policies from the middle of the eighth century—a development that looms large in the prophecies of Hosea and Isaiah—Assyria was at the height of its power under Esarhaddon (681–669 BCE) and Ashurbanipal (669–626). By the end of the latter's reign danger was knocking loudly at the door; but in 661 BCE Ashurbanipal had even sacked the Egyptian capital, Thebes. However, Egypt was to regain its independence later under Psammetichus I (664–610), the powerful founder of the 26th (Ethiopian) dynasty which was to continue well into the next century. Later, with the death of the Judaean king Josiah when he attempted to intervene to prevent Necho, the then Egyptian king, from coming to the support of Assyria, then in its death throes, Judah passed briefly under Egyptian control (609–605). However, it was the rise of the Medes as a major power and the growing strength of Babylon which presented the unanswerable challenge to Assyria. In 614 the city of Ashur fell before an alliance of Cyaxares the Mede and Nabopalassar of Babylon, and two years later, after a three years' siege, the capital city Nineveh succumbed. The year 612 BCE therefore really signals the arrival on the scene of the neo-Babylonian empire with its devastating effects on Judah. This empire was not, for all its power and influence, destined to be long-lived. In 539 the capture of Babylon by Cyrus was to herald the arrival of the Persian empire which, by contrast, was to last for two centuries.

There is another somewhat shadowy people which lurks in ancient documents and in the pages of many modern commentaries on Zephaniah and Jeremiah: the Scythians. One can say that they 'lurk' because there is not a single mention of them by name in the Old Testament, and there is very little evidence which might lead us to suppose that they were a factor in Judah and on the Egyptian border at this time. They were horse nomads who were, like the Medes, an Indo-Aryan people who had originally come from southern Russia. As the Assyrians weakened, they were no longer able to control Scythian pressure on their northern border. Herodotus (*History* 1.103) tells us that they invaded the Median kingdom during the reign of Cyaxares and that they ruled the upper country of Asia for 28 years (4.1). In 1.105 he says:

> Thence [i.e. after their attack on the Medes] they marched against Egypt, and when they were in the part of Syria called Palestine, Psammetichus king of Egypt met them and persuaded them with gifts and prayers to come no further. So they turned back...

Most scholars have met this claim with scepticism, since they regard it as unlikely that the Scythians could have done all this in the heyday of Assyrian power. However, others have thought that Jeremiah's early oracles (that is, dating from some time after his call in 626) about a threat from 'a foe from the north' may refer to them, since those oracles could hardly have referred to Babylon at that time (see Rowley). Others have wondered whether Zeph. 1.18 refers to Psammetichus's action in buying off the Scythians, and whether, as with the early Jeremiah (2.14-15), it refers to a judgment at the hand of the Scythians (see Taylor).

It is true that a recent scholar (Yamauchi) has suggested that the discovery of distinctive Scythian arrowheads in the Nile delta area offers some confirmation of Herodotus. He also finds confirmation in Millard's revised Egyptian chronology, which he used to argue that the Scythian invasion of the area followed the height of Assyrian domination. However, all this must be regarded as marginal. There are insufficient details given either by Jeremiah or Zephaniah for us to be able confidently to identify who was meant. Much more seriously, it has to be questioned whether those prophets intended to identify any particular historical power or whether they were using mythological motifs to warn of a coming judgment from God, all the more awesome for not being made specific (see Reimer). Scholars who dogmatically assume that the pre-exilic prophets always rooted their observations in particular historical circumstances are arguing in a circle in which the assumption finds justification in the supposed result.

For much of this period Judah was ruled by Manasseh, who throughout his reign (687–642 BCE) was perforce subject to the overlordship of Assyria. Our knowledge of Judah's internal affairs is dependent upon Joshua–2 Kings, a work usually known as the Deuteronomistic History (DH) because it has been shaped by editors who shared much of the theology and religious vocabulary of the book of Deuteronomy. In its final form this work appears to have been composed to explain why the disaster of the destruction of Jerusalem by Babylonian forces and the exile of the Davidic king with many of his subjects took place, in spite of God's promises that he would always defend Jerusalem, his dwelling-place, and ensure the continuance of the rule of the Davidic dynasty. It traces the cause to apostasy and religious syncretism.

The books of Chronicles also deal with the same period, but they are a late, post-exilic work which, while it may well preserve some authentic historical details in the many places where it differs from DH, is so influenced by theological concerns that it cannot be treated by itself as a reliable historical source. This has been widely recognized. What is too often overlooked by commentators when they try to determine Zephaniah's historical context is that DH is also so influenced, and that we cannot simply read it as though it were a factual, modern, history textbook.

For whatever reason, DH gives Manasseh an extremely bad

press. He is the *bête noire* of the editors (2 Kgs 21.2-18; 23.26-27). It has often been alleged that many of the aspects of foreign religion said to have been adopted by Manasseh— Canaanite Baal and Asherah worship, astral cults, child sacrifice—were forced on him by the dominant Assyrians. This theory was attacked and exploded by McKay. Nevertheless, since Yahwism was so much the national religion—one might almost say the official religion of the dynastic cult of the Davidides, providing the authority for their rule—it would not be strange if, during periods of political weakness, and thus of the ineffectiveness of a particular Davidic king, Yahwism also proved weak, and people turned to other gods for comfort and help. Allowing for the fact that this has probably led the DH editors to exaggerate Manasseh's sinfulness, one has to concede that such a period of weakness of Yahwism and of foreign influences in lifestyle and religion would correspond very well to the state of affairs attacked in Zeph. 1.4-6. The difficulty is that there were doubtless other periods in Judah's history when some justification for such attacks could be found.

Manasseh was eventually succeeded by his son Amon (642– 640 BCE), who reigned only two years before his 'servants' (palace officials, some members of the ruling classes?) assassinated him (2 Kgs 21.23). We do not know exactly who these people were and why they did this. The DH editors tell us that Amon followed the same path of religious apostasy as his father; this may mean that he followed the same pro-Assyrian political path. Some have suggested that his assassins were part of a pro-Egyptian party against whom others reacted. We simply do not know. However, the plot, whatever may have been its aim, led only to the death of the assassins at the hands of those described as 'the people of the land' who made Amon's son, Josiah, king instead.

Josiah was only eight when all this happened, and while he was a minor others must have managed the affairs of state. Just as Manasseh was the villain of the DH story so Josiah was its great hero. DH tells us that in the eighteenth year of his reign a law book was found on which he proceeded to base a thorough-going religious reform. Its aim was to purge

Yahwism of all foreign influences and of all religious syncretistic practices which denied the exclusive claims of Yahweh over his people. To this end all the outlying sanctuaries were shut down and worship was centred on the temple in Jerusalem alone (2 Kgs 23.4-24). The various enactments of this reform correspond to laws which are found in Deuteronomy; and this has led many scholars to conclude that the law book discovered in the temple was some form of the book of Deuteronomy.

Does the account in DH correspond to the facts? Chronicles tells us that the reform was a much more gradual affair which had begun already in the eighth year of Josiah's reign (2 Chron. 34.3); and this has led some to believe that DH has greatly exaggerated the effect of the 'discovery' of the law book on the reform (for example Mayes). Not so many years after the date of the reform, both Jeremiah and Ezekiel attacked the religious laxity and syncretism of their contemporaries in ways which make it difficult to believe that the reform was quite as sweeping in its effects as DH describes. Moreover, long after the exile a colony of Jewish mercenaries and their families stationed at Elephantine had an altar of their own and thought it so little irregular that they wrote to the high priest of the time in Jerusalem asking for help in rebuilding it!

A compromise view is probably best here. No doubt DH has exaggerated the nature and extent of Josiah's 'reform' and idealized the part the discovery of the law book played in it. No doubt it was fiercely resisted in some parts of the country, and much popular 'mixed' religious practice and belief continued (see not only Morton Smith, but now also M.S. Smith). The untimely death of Josiah in 609 at Megiddo when he went to oppose the advance of the Egyptian king would have led many to doubt whether he really had the blessing of Yahweh as others claimed for him and so to doubt the validity of his religious and political policies. Nevertheless, the attempt to centralize worship in Jerusalem and make Yahwism strong and exclusive has a ring of plausibility about it. With Assyrian power very much on the wane by 621, Josiah would have been free to attempt what must have been the dream of all Davidic kings from the time of Solomon onwards: to reign again over a united kingdom of Israel and Judah. Because the Davidic king ruled in the name of Yahweh, strengthening Yahwism was a way of strengthening his own hold on power. Nor must we forget the fiscal benefits to the royal exchequer of having only one place of worship to which all the tithes and temple dues were paid (cf. Oded).

Where does Zephaniah fit into all this? The superscription of the book places him in the reign of Josiah (1.1). The great majority of commentators have accepted this and have tended to place his ministry in the early, pre-reform part of that reign, because at that time the abuses of the reign of Manasseh would still be continuing. His failure to mention the king in his attacks on the ruling classes in Judah (1.8-9) might therefore be due to the fact that Josiah was a minor when policy was in the hands of others (some, as we have seen, put his silence down to his being related to Josiah). This is certainly possible, so that caution is in place. As I have said, such abuses as those which Zephaniah attacks could and did occur at other times in Judah's history, and it is by no means inconceivable that later Deuteronomistic editors wanted to claim Zephaniah's support for the reform and inserted the superscription for this purpose.

Others have argued for the Josianic period for his ministry, but *after* the reform. They see the phrase 'remnant of Baal' (1.4) as suggesting a time when Josiah's reforms had had the effect of reducing the worshippers and 'idolatrous priests' of Baal to a mere handful. This might, but need not, be so. The phrase might be merely contemptuous; 1.2-4 does not in fact suggest the minority practice of a handful of die-hards, but rather a thriving religious industry. Others have seen the phrase 'the king's sons' (1.8) as referring to Josiah's sons and so as related to a later stage of his life. But, like the phrase 'sons of the prophets' referring to a group in general, the phrase may refer to the royal retinue of the palace. One recent commentator who favours this post-reform era in Josiah's reign is O. Palmer Robertson: he believes that the strong parallels with Deuteronomic language suggest a time after the discovery of the law book in 621. Again, this is possible, but a 'Deuteronomic movement' must have been at work before that time; and, as we have seen, Zephaniah could well have been part of that.

D.L. Williams believes that Jehoiakim's reign (609–598) provides the best context for Zephaniah's activity. Jehoiakim was placed on the throne in 609 by the Egyptians when, following the death of Josiah, Judah fell for a while under their control. They deposed his brother Jehoahaz who had briefly followed Josiah. However, Williams's arguments are tenuous. He thinks it unlikely that the Scythians came as far as the Egyptian border, and therefore that Zephaniah's threats of judgment from Yahweh in the form of enemy attack best fit the Babylonian advance which became a lively threat only at this time. Since Zephaniah is quite unspecific this is necessarily an assumption. Williams believes that the threat to Nineveh (2.13-15) shows a knowledge of its fall in 612 BCE, and that it constitutes 'prophecy after the event'. This is possible; but any prophet of the time would have had many examples of sacked cities with which to fill out an imaginative account. Williams identifies the prophet Zephaniah with the priest Zephaniah (2 Kgs 25.18-21/Jer. 52.24ff.) who was deported by the Babylonians—an assumption without any evidence to support it. For him, the conditions described by Zephaniah best fit the time after the death of Josiah when disillusion followed the failure of his policies.

All this shows not only the weakness of the arguments for dating Zephaniah in the reign of Jehoiakim but also the weakness of *any* attempts to date him by alleged historical references in a book in which they by no means appear on the surface. The main interest of the book is not historical. This is also true of attempts to find supposed historical allusions in the oracles against the nations in ch. 2, such as that of Christensen who assumes that these oracles form a literary whole in their present form and that 'a single historical situation in c. 628 makes an excellent setting for all of the historical allusions in question'. There are in fact no clear historical allusions in these oracles. They contain some accusations and some quite general threats; and, as they stand, they have been broadened out into examples of particular sins which will always bring Yahweh's judgment. The aim is theological, not historical; and, as the book stands, these oracles are clearly meant to relate to the fortunes of God's own people either by way of example, warning or contrast.

One extreme effort to 'date' the book of Zephaniah was that of L.P. Smith and E.L. Lacheman who argued that the book as it stands shows apocalyptic ideas and language which are reminiscent of Ezekiel and Second Isaiah and which, in places, parallel the book of Daniel. These authors believe that 1.4-13 is an old oracle which originated in the sixth century, but that the extension of this in 1.14-18 to *all* the earth shows parallels with later, post-exilic literature; and that the apocalyptic elements of chs. 2 and 3 place the book around the era of 200 BCE, near the time of the book of Daniel. The difficulty with such attempts to date by literary parallels is to know which way round the influences work. It is, of course, by no means impossible that there are post-exilic passages in the book (there is nothing which warrants so late a date as Smith and Lacheman give), but do parallels with Ezekiel and Second Isaiah occur because these influenced Zephaniah, or because Zephaniah influenced them, or, much more likely, because both drew from common source material and from the same general influences as those offered by the pre-exilic temple worship of Jerusalem?

Conclusions must, therefore, be modest. Zephaniah, as far as we can tell, would fit very well with the general feeling for political and religious reform which, when the time was ripe, gave rise to the whole Deuteronomic movement and the reforms of Josiah. Equally, we have to allow that the strictures in the book are so general and 'historical' allusions so imprecise that it could fit a whole range of other historical contexts. No doubt, however, Zephaniah's words and warnings could have continued to be used in the very difficult times which followed Josiah's death, when the temptation to abandon strict Yahwism would have been great for many people. It is entirely probable that the 'Deuteronomists' during the exile would have claimed Zephaniah for the reform, and that his prophecies would have underlined their own theological message: that the fall of Jerusalem and the Babylonian exile happened because of the people's religious faithlessness. Even after the exile we know that the words of the earlier prophets were used as 'texts' by which to exhort and encourage the faithful (for example Zech. 1.4). It is probably a mistake to attempt to isolate a prophet, and certainly a prophetic book, in one historical context alone. Whoever he was and whenever he lived, tradition saw him as a much more universal figure who went on speaking to each successive generation; and the book reflects this belief. The force of his message for their own day was the readers' concern, not his personal biography or the history of the times in which he lived.

Further Reading

D.L. Christensen, 'Zeph. 2:4-15: A Theological Basis for Josiah's Program of Political Expansion', *CBQ* 46 (1984), pp. 669-82.

J. McKay, *Religion in Judah under the Assyrians* (SBT 2nd ser., 26; London: SCM Press, 1973).

A.D.H. Mayes, *Deuteronomy* (NCB; London: Marshall, Morgan & Scott, 1979).

A.R. Millard, 'The Scythian Problem', in J. Ruffle *et al.* (eds.), *Glimpses of Ancient Egypt* (Warminster, 1979), pp. 119-22.

B. Oded, 'Judah and the Exile', in J.H. Hayes and J.M. Miller (eds.), *Israelite and Judean History* (London: SCM Press, 1977), pp. 435-88.

D. Reimer, 'The "Foe" and the "North" in Jeremiah', *ZAW* 101 (1989), pp. 223-32.

Robertson, *The Books of Nahum, Habakkuk and Zephaniah*.

H.H. Rowley, 'The Early Prophecies of Jeremiah in their Setting', *BJRL* 45 (1962–63), pp. 198-234 (repr. in *Men of God* [London: Nelson, 1963], pp. 133-68).

L.P. Smith and E.L. Lacheman, 'The Authorship of Zephaniah', *JNES* 9 (1950), pp. 137-42.

M. Smith, *Palestinian Parties and Politics that Shaped the Old Testament* (New York: Columbia University Press, 1971).

M.S. Smith, *The Early History of God* (San Francisco: Harper & Row, 1990).

Taylor, 'Zephaniah'.

D.L. Williams, 'The Date of Zephaniah', *JBL* 82 (1963), pp. 77-88.

E. Yamauchi, 'The Scythians: Invading Hordes from the Russian Steppes', *BA* 46 (1983), pp. 90-99.

6
THE HISTORY OF CRITICISM

AS WITH THE STUDY OF other prophetic books it is possible to detect in broad terms three different ways in which critical scholars have approached the text of Zephaniah. Older study concerned itself with determining what parts of the book came from an historical prophet, Zephaniah, and what had been added later. Such additions were often referred to as 'glosses' and were understood as editorial comments designed to help later generations to understand certain references better or to see the point of the prophet's words for their own day. Words like 'authentic' and 'inauthentic' were often used, suggesting a rather negative attitude towards the glossators' efforts. Additions were identified by the criteria of differences of vocabulary, style and thought, and by the comparison of particular passages with other Old Testament texts known, or supposed, to be late. Many commentators also rejected certain poetic lines on metrical grounds. Such methods continue to be used, and often underlie newer approaches.

More recently there has been greater interest in the process by which these later elements have been combined with the prophet's words and in the reasons behind that process. Special attention has been paid to the activity of later editors or 'redactors' (hence the term 'redaction criticism'). Together with this has gone an interest in the structure or *form* of the various components of the book (form criticism) and in the various themes or 'motifs' that can be detected in each of its layers. More recently, sometimes in reaction to what has been seen as the over-analytical interests of these earlier methods, attention has been directed to 'the final form' of the book. Such study has concerned itself with the intentions of those who gave us the book in its present shape, reminding us that they intended it to be read as a whole.

I have already indicated some of the verses which various scholars have thought to be later additions to the book of Zephaniah. It would be tedious to try to summarize exactly what each scholar has rejected and why. At different times, almost every verse in the book has been questioned! It has generally been felt, however, that the heart of Zephaniah's message is to be found in ch. 1 with its indictment of the religious syncretism of the people and priests in Judah and Jerusalem, the way of life of many of its leaders and the religious scepticism and apathy of its prosperous merchants. All of these are threatened with a coming 'Day of Yahweh' which is seen in terms familiar from Amos and Isaiah as a day of darkness and distress for God's people. But some have questioned vv. 2-3, and more vv. 17-18 which seem to project such threats into a universal, cosmic judgment of all people throughout the whole earth (for example Pfeiffer, Elliger, Fohrer, Kaiser). On the other hand, R.L. Smith has pointed out that Micah and Amos both begin with a broader concern before addressing Israel in particular.

Of the oracles against the nations in ch. 2 much has been contested at one stage or another. Beer questioned vv. 1-3, and J.M.P. Smith saw v. 3 as secondary since it breaks the sequence of vv. 2 and 4 and of the 'lament' metrical rhythm. Wellhausen held that vv. 2-3 are both dubious, while Schwally saw all of vv. 5-12 as an exilic addition. Many have felt that vv. 8-11 reflect the gratitude felt by many of Israel's neighbours when Israel was defeated by Babylon, while even some who believed that a seventh-century prophet might have spoken against Moab and Ammon held that references to 'repossession' of the territory of former enemies by a Judaean 'remnant' in vv. 7 and 9 express a later, post-exilic hope. The idea in v. 11 of Yahweh's triumph over other gods was felt by some to echo Second Isaiah's views and so to be exilic or post-exilic (so, for example, Renaud).

There has been a great deal of support for the view that

much of ch. 3 is post-exilic. Wellhausen dismissed the whole chapter as late, while J.M.P. Smith saw all of vv. 8-13 as post-exilic. These verses, however, were not themselves unitary. Verses 8-9 were, according to Smith, an even later gloss which showed a different attitude towards the nations from that evident in vv. 6 and 11. A great many have seen 3.14-20 as a late, almost apocalyptic picture of Yahweh's final victory as universal king, its language and imagery having been drawn from the Enthronement Psalms and from Second Isaiah. The final picture of a returned Jewish 'diaspora' in vv. 19-20 was held to reflect a later stage still in Judah's history.

However, some scholars have argued for a much greater unity in the book, attributing it to Zephaniah himself; and these are not confined to the theologically 'conservative'. C.A. Keller divides the book into nine sections, finding three discourses of Yahweh, four of the prophet and two in which the words of the prophet are completed by words of Yahweh. The familiar prophetic scheme of oracles against Judah, oracles against the nations and oracles of salvation can be seen; yet the book breaks out of this scheme, since the unifying theme of the 'Day of Yahweh' embraces both Israel and the nations in its effects. Except for a few glosses, Keller thinks that the whole book is authentic apart from 18aβ-20, and he dates the prophet, from the religious and political circumstances presupposed, about 625 BCE.

An example of the interests and methods of redaction criticism is offered by Renaud. He rejects the usual threefold structure of the book based on the subject matter of the three chapters (judgment against Judah, judgment against the nations and salvation for Judah) because the first section contains visions of *universal* judgment, not merely judgment against Judah; the oracles against the nations include words about the 'remnant' and are concerned also with Judah's future; and 3.1-7 develops the idea of the condemnation of Jerusalem, while v. 8 offers a new perspective of universal judgment. He sees the book as structured by a recurrence at strategic points of the generalizing expression 'In the fire of my/his jealousy, all the earth shall be consumed' (1.18; 3.8). This gives a threefold structure to the book, but one which is different from that which has usually been accepted. The unifying theme is 'the Day of Yahweh'. 1.2-18 describes that day as one of radical, universal judgment, while 3.9-20 shows it to be one of conversion and peace. The second part (2.1–3.8) exhibits a contrast to both of these aspects and yet establishes their coherence. It refers to the existence in Judah of a remnant who will survive the judgment and become the new eschatological people.

Renaud sees at least three stages in the composition of the book, although each may be itself the result of a complex process of growth. He sees first the remains of the message of a seventh-century prophet, Zephaniah, who, in the manner of Amos and Isaiah, predicted a 'Day of Yahweh' of judgment against Judah and Jerusalem especially because of the behaviour of the religious, social and political leaders. The core of this prediction is found in 1.4-16, though here there are traces of a second 'Deuteronomistic' layer of glossed comments such as v. 6. Zephaniah himself may also have issued the call for repentance in 2.1-3 and some of the oracles against the nations. Possibly he also saw the hope of salvation for a remnant, if 3.11-13 is original. Such a prophet, with the picture he paints of society, would fit well into the time before, or early in, the period of Josiah's reform which Renaud, favouring the Chronicler's account, tends to see as having extended over something like a ten-year period. He must have been a conservative Yahwist who showed real sympathy for 'the little people' of society. He had some contact with the Wisdom writers and also with the Deuteronomists, although his chief sources of inspiration were the prophets Amos and Isaiah. If Israel would take warning from the fate of the nations and repent, there was a chance that they might know God's pardon.

After the Deuteronomistic redaction, apparent in a number of individual glosses, the main shape of the book came, according to Renaud, from the hand of a post-exilic, sixth- or fifth-century redactor, whose influence is seen in the present tripartite shape of the book. In 1.2-3 and 14-16 this redactor gave the 'Day of Yahweh' theme a universal dimension encompassing both Judah and the nations. In the second part he took several originally disparate elements and developed them into the same theme. These included the appeal for conversion (2.1-3) and the oracles against the nations, together with the indictment of Jerusalem (3.1-7). In this way he also united Judah and the nations in God's whole purpose of judgment and salvation. In 2.15 an original oracle against Nineveh has been placed so as to refer to both that city and Jerusalem. Another element was introduced by this editor in 2.7, 9b-10, which sees the 'remnant of Judah' as ultimately triumphant over its enemies. In the third part a similar 'universalizing' tendency is at work. An oracle of Zephaniah in 3.11-13a directed towards Jerusalem has been supplemented in 3.9-10 by one relating to the nations. 3.9-20 as a whole has been arranged by this redactor in three sections (vv. 9-13, 14-18a, 18b-20), each elaborating the theme of 'at this time' or 'in that day' in order to end the whole collection on a note of hope of Yahweh's universal reign.

Two related studies may be briefly mentioned. H. Irsigler carried out an elaborate and detailed literary-critical examination of 1.1–2.3. He isolated seven sections, among which he distinguished those in the form of direct speech of Yahweh from those which are reported as words of the prophet. The former announce Yahweh's judgment, while the latter show how the prophet elaborated this into his theme of a 'Day of Yahweh' which was universal in its scope. Irsigler too believed that 2.1-3, with its call for repentance and its distinction between the true 'poor' and the unfaithful, was addressed by the final redactor to the post-exilic community.

In 1977 G. Krinetzki published an investigation into the book which combined a traditional historical-critical approach with a redaction-critical approach and a study of the book's main themes. In a detailed study he isolated certain oracles from Zephaniah which he dated variously between 639 and 620 BCE (while admitting that some could not be dated with certainty). One of these came from a disciple (2.8-9) between 602 and 587 while three were of unknown authorship (2.5-6, 3.14-15, 16-18a, and 3.18b-19[20]). This collection combining the prophet's oracles with those which he inspired was then subjected to two main redactional stages. The first came from

Deuteronomistic circles in the first half of the sixth century
BCE, and was responsible for the superscription of the book
(1.1) and for the placing of 1.7 in its present position (it had
originally introduced vv. 14-18). Other marks of this stage are
to be found mainly in interpretative glosses and 'redactional
elements', such as the word 'for' at the beginning of 2.4a and
some introductory phrases such as 'on that day' as in 3.11a.
The second redaction dated from near the end of the fourth
century BCE; its particular interest was a concern for the
return of the Jewish Diaspora (for example in 2.7, 9; 3.10b,
18b-19 and 20).

All this study is necessary and no doubt reflects, in general,
something of what must have happened in the production of
any prophetic book. However, the methods, yielding as they
do such widely varying results, must be seen to contain a
subjective element. Results are bound to stem from the pre-
suppositions we bring to the text. We have only the one, final
form of this text from which to work. A.S. Kapelrud makes a
good point when he says that some of the units left to the
prophet when critics have finished their work of analysis are
so short that it is difficult to imagine their being uttered in
any kind of context or with any sort of intelligibility. He
protests against seeing what he calls 'rhetorical units' (the
usually small units identified by form critics whose beginning
and end are marked with formulae such as 'Thus says the
LORD' or 'Oracle of the LORD') as complete 'speeches' in
themselves. The prophets would have used these, he argues,
but worked them into longer and more coherent rhetorical
units. Kapelrud claims that the prophets varied between one
poetic metre and another and used repetitions and abrupt
changes of form. Speaking of 1.7–2.3 he says:

> All these methods can be observed within the unit...but in spite
> of the use of different metres and different rhetorical means it is
> nevertheless one speech, kept together by a terrifying content:
> close at hand is the Day of Yahweh.

I have written elsewhere about the limitations of redaction
criticism as a method. While it recognizes the truth that all of
our biblical books have undergone long and complex processes
of development consisting of reshaping, reinterpretation and

reapplication in new situations, it can detect this only in very general terms. Claims to be able, for example, to date the redactional level of the word 'for' and of 'In that day' break the bounds of credibility. It is because of this that, more recently, a number of scholars have directed their attention to the final form of the book. We have to take seriously, they claim, the intentions of those who were responsible for its ultimate shape. I will complete this section by mentioning the work of two of these scholars (although the work of those who find a unity in the book by virtue of its cultic background also needs to be remembered; see above).

P.R. House has been strongly influenced by contemporary methods of literary criticism. Impatient with the methods and results of traditional Old Testament criticism, he insists that we must examine a work such as the book of Zephaniah for the signs it gives of literary genre. These he finds in alternating speeches between Yahweh and the prophet which depict the unfolding of a plot involving conflict and resolution. The theme of this 'plot' is that of 'the day of Yahweh'; and it can be traced in three 'acts' each having two or three 'scenes'. Act 1 (1.2-17) comprises three scenes entitled 'General Judgment and Explanation' (1.2-7), 'Judgment of Judah and Explanation' (1.8-16) and 'Yahweh's Closing Soliloquy' (1.17). The three scenes of Act 2 (1.18–3.5) are 'The Prophet's Soliloquy of Judgment and Hope' (1.18–2.7), 'More Judgment and Hope in which both Yahweh and the Prophet Speak' (2.8–2.11) and 'Final Threats' (2.12–3.5), dominated by words of the prophet after a brief statement by Yahweh against the Ethiopians in 2.12. Act 3 consists of 'The Resolution in Scene 1 (3.6-17) which is shared by Yahweh and the prophet, and Yahweh's closing soliloquy in Scene 2 (3.18-20).

Such an imaginative approach, which insists that we look at the work as a whole, is refreshing, and certainly has a contribution to make to Zephaniah studies. We are now being constantly reminded that there is no such thing as a completely objective reading of the text, and that there are as many legitimate responses to a text as there are readers of that text. Liberation theology readings, feminist readings and a whole variety of other readings all have something to contribute to our appreciation of the sweep and power of any given text, as Rogerson has recently reminded us in examining various ways in which the early chapters of Genesis have been read. In a recent survey of scholarly studies of the book of Zephaniah, E. Ball, while insisting that we take seriously 'the complex redactional patterning of the material', welcomes attempts to read it as a literary whole and adds:

> When we seek to take into account the profound theological issues and affirmations embodied in it, it is salutory to ask whether we (whoever 'we' are!) do in fact know how to read such a prophetic book.

However, it would be a mistake to insist that we must use one approach to the exclusion of others. We must go on trying as best we can (with all the limitations and imperfections of our methods and our acknowledged subjective preconceptions) to discover what the text was meant to say to its contemporaries. It would be quite wrong to imagine that the old methods of text, form and redaction criticism are all 'subjective' while such an approach as House's is 'objective'. He does not ask how all this disparate material with its obvious unevenness of thought and style has been combined to create a dramatic whole. Presumably some unknown 'final editor' did this; but this question does not interest House. Further, features which he alleges make the work a 'drama' are by no means peculiar to this book. As we have seen, most of the prophetic books present the 'drama' of judgment against Israel and judgment against the nations with a final resolution of salvation and the triumph of Yahweh's plans. In almost all the prophetic books, oracles of first-person divine speech alternate with third-person oracles of the prophet. It is not always obvious that there is great significance in these changes or in the order in which they occur.

One can question House's arrangement at a number of points. For example, in 1.6, 'those who turn away from Yahweh and do not seek the Lord nor inquire of him' (House's translation) is placed in a first-person divine speech of Yahweh. Again, in 1.10, 'It shall be on that day says Yahweh, a cry will come from the Fish Gate...' is assigned to a speech by Yahweh himself, but the very similar construction in 2.5,

'The word of Yahweh is against you, O Canaan, land of the Philistine, I will destroy you' is included in a speech of the prophet. Further, it is extremely difficult to see the exact dramatic effect of the very uneven alternation of speeches of Yahweh and the prophet in these scenes. We have nothing here like the dialogue offered by for example the book of Job, which could be described with much greater plausibility as a 'drama'. All this is not said to deny the worth and legitimacy of such final form readings; it is urged rather against the view that this is somehow the final answer for biblical criticism of which all other methods have been but the first stumbling steps of preparation. Ehud ben Zvi offers wise counsel in this connection:

> The historical-critical methods in biblical studies at their best may provide only probable (i.e., not yet falsified) hypotheses concerning biblical societies, their literature, and their religious thought. The alternative to the historical-critical methods is either a plethora of hypotheses without any publicly-known and critical criteria on which to assign validity, or a self-centred reading of the text, in which there is one standard: the conceptual world of the reader, be it individual or communal.

My final example of reading the book as a whole is that of ben Zvi himself. In many ways his detailed and lengthy examination of the book could be described as redaction criticism, although it incorporates a great deal of earlier historical-critical method as well. His work leads him to a result that deserves particular consideration. Like many redaction critics he sees three levels in the book which he describes as (1) 'pre-compositional', to which (2) some isolated 'post-compositional' units have been added. As this suggests, however, he sees the book as we have it (3) as a post-exilic composition, and treats it as such. The main thrust of ben Zvi's argument concerns the outlook and theology of the unknown post-exilic author (all the language points to ben Zvi's seeing the work in mainly literary terms); although, a little confusingly, he is not prepared to posit only a single author. This concession might leave us with a vague idea of something written by a committee, were it not made clear that he sees the production of the book as a continuing process in which the text was considered 'open' over a considerable period of time. What is clear, however, is that he finds only a few 'pre-compositional' elements, and these are themselves too varied to enable us to attribute them to a single prophet. We therefore know nothing whatever from the book of a historical prophet called Zephaniah, nor is such a hypothetical figure of any interest or significance to us. Not Zephaniah but 'the word of Yahweh' is at the centre of the book. Such pictures as we are given are not of any flesh and blood pre-exilic prophet but of an idealized figure who delivers sophisticated speeches and calls for repentance. Since no attempt is made by ben Zvi to anchor the book in any particular historical context (the super-scription merely shows the view of the author that such a message would have been suitable in a time of reform such as Josiah's) and none of the traditional characteristics of a prophet is attributed to Zephaniah, we may assume that the author(s) may even have been opposed to those who claimed to be prophets in their own day. These found their inspiration certainly in past prophetic teaching, but also in the Wisdom writers and, above all, in the *anawim* psalms (psalms about 'the poor'). This may suggest that they saw themselves as oppressed by wealthy, wicked and impious enemies, and that they identified themselves with those described in 2.3 as 'the humble of the land'. They evinced no interest in any messianic deliverer figure and they called for no military or political action, so they were probably quietists who found hope in waiting for the ultimate deliverance of Yahweh who alone is righteous.

Like those of any of these writers, some of ben Zvi's methods and assumptions are questionable. He usually assigns material to one composition level or another by its parallels in other biblical literature which can often be shown to be seventh century, exilic or post-exilic. He can say, 'It is note-worthy that this evidence of parallels exists despite the relatively small corpus of written works in our hands'. In fact, however, it can by no means be assumed that because a certain word, phrase or idea occurs elsewhere, say in a seventh-century work, it is therefore itself of the seventh cen-tury. Writers use familiar vocabulary and traditional ideas, even where they creatively rework the material. Ben Zvi often seems to be using such methods almost mechanically, certainly too literally. Not all will be able to share the confidence with which he often claims to be able to 'date' a verse or part-verse.

Nevertheless, ben Zvi's emphasis is a most useful one. Like almost all the prophetic books, Zephaniah, as we have it, is a post-exilic book, and can only be read intelligibly when we recognize this and liberate ourselves from exclusive preoccupation with unearthing the actual words of a particular historical prophet, as I have argued elsewhere in the case of the book of Micah. Even so, we must not exclude efforts to see how the book developed; for by such efforts, however imperfectly we succeed, we shall understand more clearly the aims and methods of the later, post-exilic redactors. Both the witness of the prophet and the interpretation of the redactors are part of the riches of the book as we have it, and our understanding will be diminished if we undervalue the contribution of either.

Further Reading

E. Ball, 'Zephaniah', in R.J. Coggins and J.L. Houlden (eds.), *A Dictionary of Biblical Interpretation* (London: SCM Press; Philadelphia: Trinity Press International, 1990), pp. 742-43.

P.R. House, *Zephaniah: A Prophetic Drama* (JSOTSup, 69; Sheffield: JSOT Press, 1988).

H. Irsigler, *Gottesgericht und Yahwetag* (St Ottilien: Eos Verlag, 1977).

A.S. Kapelrud, *The Message of the Prophet Zephaniah: Morphology and Ideas* (Oslo: Universitets-forlaget, 1975).

Keller, *Michée, Nahoum, Habakuk, Sophonie.*

G. Krinetzki, *Zephanjastudien: Motive- und Traditionskritik + Kompositions- und Redaktionskritik* (Frankfurt: Peter Lang, 1977).

R.A. Mason, *Micah, Nahum, Obadiah* (OTG; Sheffield: JSOT Press, 1991).

Renaud, *Michée, Sophonie, Nahoum.*

J. Rogerson, *Genesis 1-11* (OTG; Sheffield: JSOT Press, 1991).

F. Schwally, 'Das Buch Ssefanjä, eine historische-kritische Untersuchung', *ZAW* 10 (1890), pp. 165-240.

Smith, *Micah–Malachi.*

E. ben Zvi, *A Historical–Critical Study of the Book of Zephaniah* (BZAW, 198; Giessen: Töpelmann, 1991).

7

THE MESSAGE OF ZEPHANIAH

THE BOOK OF ZEPHANIAH is one of the most politically, socially and religiously radical of the prophetic books of the Old Testament. It is anti-establishment to a degree which would make a liberation theology reading of it quite understandable. As we have seen, it is not possible to say confidently just which parts of it came from a seventh-century prophet called Zephaniah and which are to be seen as later interpretation and reapplication of his message. But it would be unduly sceptical to suppose that a tradition could have arisen which had no initiator and no individual to give it its particular insight, one which at many points, it is true, echoes that of other prophetic books, but which in its presentation shows marked individuality. To posit an individual in this way is of course to make an assumption, but it is an assumption more plausible than the view that later anonymous writers created the prophet *ex nihilo* in their own image.

In attacking not just religious syncretism, which combined the worship of Yahweh with the worship of other deities, but apostasy, in which the worshippers substituted other gods for Yahweh (1.4-6), Zephaniah shows something of the outlook of those who were preparing the reforms of Josiah, the soil in which the Deuteronomic movement was nourished. For reasons given above it seems more likely that such attacks preceded the reform itself. But Zephaniah combines criticism of cultic apostasy with indignation against the social injustice by which the rich and powerful exploit the poor, thereby combining the separate emphases of Amos and Hosea. It is the members of the palace retinue, the foppish and effete rich, the capitalist traders, those whose wealth has made them complacent and insensitive to the faith and to the spiritual values and moral insights of religion, who are attacked (1.8-9, 11-12). In the Day of Yahweh which is coming, a day envisaged in the Amos/Isaiah tradition as a day of darkness, of reversal of fortunes, of the overturning of the status quo, it is particularly the 'mighty' and the whole organized system of 'the city' that will feel its brunt (1.14-16). It is quite probable that vv. 1.2-4 and 17-19 represent a later development of this thought, extending the original threat against seventh-century Jerusalem to the wider world in which the post-exilic Jewish communities, both in Judah and in 'the Diaspora', suffer and are oppressed. Yet even here it is those who have 'the silver and the gold' to make them secure in their power who are singled out for judgment (1.18). In the reversal of the original act of creation (1.2-3), those who smugly see their role as the 'rulers' of the earth (cf. Gen. 1.26-28, where such dominion is given to Adam and Eve, i.e. to humankind, a word significantly found here in 1.3d) will have their supremacy taken away from them, as has been rightly seen by the glossator who has added in v. 3 the comment, 'I will overthrow the wicked'.

It is impossible to know whether Zephaniah uttered any or all of the oracles against the nations since, as we have already seen, no historical details remain, if any were there in the first instance. These oracles have, however, been 'generalized' to illustrate, as in 1.2-4 and 17-19, that the just judgment of God will fall on all who oppress the righteous and the poor, with their 'taunts' and 'boasts' (2.8, 10), their contempt of Yahweh in their treatment of his people, and their 'pride' (2.10). The fate threatened against Jerusalem in 1.10-13 will befall every oppressive city, typified here by Nineveh with its arrogance (2.13-15). But just as Second Isaiah saw that exiled Israel would be redeemed and brought back because of Yahweh's supreme power over every other god, so the same ground of assurance is given here (2.11).

In the renewed attack on Jerusalem (3.1-5) it is again the figures of the religious and political 'establishment' that are singled out (vv. 3-5). They will be ejected from office because they have been false representatives of the God in whose name they claimed to rule, failing to realize that when he hears the appeals of the poor and dispenses justice 'in the morning' he does so in righteousness and in utter integrity (3.5). If 1.4-16 comes from Zephaniah there is no logical reason why 3.1-5 should not also be his. The establishment should have learned from God's wider, universal judgment against wickedness wherever it is found, and so should have taken action in time (3.6-8). Presumably the same hand is responsible for this note as that which has 'generalized' the oracles against the nations in ch. 2. Indeed, it is regarded as by no means impossible here that foreigners who learned from God's judgment would 'enter the kingdom' before 'the proudly exultant ones' in Jerusalem.

This introduces another note which has already been implicit in the singling out of the leaders for attack. In this corrupt and oppressive society there are those who can be described in the language of the Psalms as the 'humble', the 'lowly' and the 'poor'. For such people the 'Day of Yahweh', which brings the downfall of every oppressive and corrupt political tyrant, will bring deliverance. As the 'remnant' they will, like the 'meek' of the beatitudes, 'inherit the earth' (2.7, 9). Such people have long since learned not to put their trust in princes. There is no mention here of a messianic deliverer of the Davidic or any other royal line. Their only king, as also their only hope, is God; the rich language and imagery of the worship of the pre-exilic temple whose liturgy is found in the Psalms celebrating Yahweh's kingship are drawn on to express their hope of victory (3.14-20). This, which will be bad news for the rich and powerful, will be good news for 'the lame and the outcast' (3.19). It is they who then will be truly valued and honoured in the new moral perspectives of the kingdom of God.

The words of Zephaniah to the faithful of seventh-century Judah who were appalled at what they saw and oppressed because of what they suffered have become here a kind of charter of hope and faith for the oppressed and rejected of the post-exilic age and, indeed, of every age. This little book witnesses to the kingship of God as powerfully as any other in the Old Testament. It is not, to be sure, a call to the political path of revolution. But it is nevertheless revolutionary. It passes sentence of death on the oppressive kingdoms of this world, and witnesses to the ultimate truth that they will become the kingdoms of God. It is therefore a call to faith and endurance on the part of the oppressed. Who is to say, however, that their patient, quiet witness to the ultimate victory of justice does not have as explosive a final effect as the bloodier path of revolution?

Part II

HABAKKUK

8
THE CONTENTS OF THE BOOK OF HABAKKUK

IN 1977 THE GERMAN scholar P. Jöcken published a detailed and comprehensive history of investigation of the book of Habakkuk. Towards the end of this he wrote, with perhaps just a hint of justifiable pride, that he had surveyed over 150 years of scholarly study of the book, and mentioned the work of more than 300 scholars. If he were now to issue a revised edition he would have to take note of many more articles, books and commentaries, with little sign of the flood drying to a trickle. And yet the book consists of only three chapters, and the main outline of its contents and their division into units is fairly clear and uncontroversial. The interpretation of these units, however, their relation to each other, their form and function, their historical context or contexts, the redactional process which has brought them to their present order, the role and identity of the 'prophet' Habakkuk himself, have all proved a veritable minefield for critical study. Any critic bold enough to step out firmly across this danger area is likely to find hidden traps or, at least, to come under a fusillade of crossfire from scholarly peers. It seems safest, therefore, to begin cautiously with a description of the book's contents.

Habakkuk 1.1

The book begins with a superscription, describing Habakkuk as a prophet and using a conventional prophetic formula, 'The word/oracle ($d\bar{a}b\bar{a}r$) which X saw...' (cf. Amos 1.1; Isa. 1.1; 2.1; 13.1). Less usual is the absence of any details giving a historical context for the prophet's activity such as 'in the days of X, king of Judah' (cf. Isa. 1.1; Jer. 1.1-3; Ezek. 1.2; Hos. 1.1; Amos 1.1; Mic. 1.1; Zeph. 1.1; Hag. 1.1; Zech. 1.1). It may or may not be significant that the other prophetic books in which such details are lacking (Joel, Obadiah, Nahum, Malachi) are those which some scholars have thought to have particular associations with the cultic worship of the temple. However, such matters have to be decided in each case on the basis of the form and contents of the books rather than on the shape of the later, editorial superscriptions. Elliger, for example, suggests that the lack of any such details in the superscription might show that at least the core of the collection was formed in the prophet's lifetime, so rendering them unnecessary.

Habakkuk 1.2-4

These verses consist of 'lament' or 'complaint' of the prophet, showing strong parallels with some psalms of similar form and contents (for example Pss. 10, 13), questioning the delay in God's answer to the prophet's call for divine intervention in a situation of social injustice, violence and conflict. (See Day, *The Psalms*, for a recent examination of this type of psalm.)

Habakkuk 1.5-11

These verses form an oracle, expressed in first-person divine speech, announcing that God is about to do an astonishing work by 'raising' the Chaldeans (Babylonians). Their power and frightening military prowess is described. The use by Yahweh of foreign powers to be the agents of his work, either of judgment or deliverance for his own people, is a familiar prophetic theme in the Old Testament, although here exactly what God is sending them to do is not specified.

Habakkuk 1.12-17

This passage is a second lament by the prophet, identified as such by his second-person address to God. Here it is explicitly stated that God is bringing 'them' (the Babylonians?) for judgment, but this appears to raise difficulties for the prophet. How can God, who is just, look on passively while the wicked and faithless destroy those more righteous than themselves? (This paraphrase disguises a strange alternation in the Hebrew between the singular and plural.) Again the excessive cruelty of the enemy is described, and the final question of the prophet is whether he is to be allowed to continue like this for ever (or 'without mercy'; see Cathcart).

Habakkuk 2.1-5

This is a second oracle, set in a narrative account by the prophet describing how he takes up his position like a watchman on a lookout post. A similar picture of the prophet as a 'watchman' looking out for the first signs of news of Yahweh's deliverance is found in Isa. 21.8-12. Here God tells the prophet to write the vision down in large characters on a tablet (cf. Isa. 30.8) and to wait in faith for its outcome even if its fulfilment seems long delayed. The answer given contains words made even more familiar by St Paul's quotation of them in Rom. 1.17: 'The righteous shall live by his faithfulness'. As we shall see, the extent and exact meaning of this oracle have been much discussed, but in the context it is clearly meant to be a word of divine reassurance in answer to the complaints of the prophet.

Habakkuk 2.6-20

This passage consists of a series of five 'woes', or prophetic imprecations against the wicked. (The point of transition from the preceding section is not quite clear, and some have made the break in v. 5b.) This culminates in an assurance that God is in the temple with all the earth called to silence before him. That this was a familiar cultic cry for 'silence' before a theophany is suggested by its appearance also in Zeph. 1.7, and Zech. 2.13 [2.17]).

Habakkuk 3.1-19

This passage contains a 'prayer' of Habakkuk. This is what it is called in its superscription; and this, together with the musical directions provided at the beginning and the end of the passage, suggests a parallel with some of the Psalms (for example Pss. 7, 61). The prayer begins (v. 2) by recalling God's work in the past and perhaps praying for its renewal in the present (but see M. Barré and R.D. Haak). It then describes (vv. 3-7) a divine theophany from the south (cf. Judg. 5.4-5; Deut. 33.2; Ps. 68.7-10[8-11]). Another section (vv. 8-15) describes God's victory in mythological terms reminiscent of the description of Ba'al's victory over Prince Yam in the Canaanite Ugaritic literature (see Day, *God's Conflict with the Dragon and the Sea*). The prayer ends (vv. 16-19) with a further description of the prophet patiently waiting for this divine intervention and with the assurance that his faith will yet be vindicated.

Questions Posed by the Book

Despite the apparently straightforward structure of the book of Habakkuk, it has as I noted above created much controversy among critics. Major areas of dispute include the following:

1. Who are the 'wicked' and the 'righteous' (see 1.4, 13; 2.4)? Are they 'wicked' native Judaean oppressors or are they foreigners? Is the singular form of these nouns in each case a 'collective singular' or does it refer to a particular individual?

2. Do these terms have the same meaning in each of the passages mentioned above, or may they refer to different groups, or to a different individual, in each context?

3. How are the different sections related to each other? Why are there two prophetic complaints with two answering oracles? What is the significance of the 'woes' and of their placing after the second oracle? Is

the psalm of ch. 3 integrally related to the book as a whole and, if so, is this relationship original or is the psalm a later addition relevant to the whole only in the book's final form?

4. What was the historical context of the book and of the prophet?

5. Are there any discernible signs of a redactional process within the present form of the book whereby material which originally related to one historical context has been later adapted to another?

In the next chapter I shall begin to trace the paths which different commentators have attempted to steer through these critical issues.

Further Reading

M. Barré, 'Habakkuk 3:2: Translation in Context', *CBQ* 50 (1988), pp. 184-97.

J. Cathcart, 'A New Proposal for Hab. 1:17', *Bib* 65 (1984), pp. 575-76.

J. Day, *God's Conflict with the Dragon and the Sea* (Cambridge: Cambridge University Press, 1985).

—*The Psalms* (OTG; Sheffield: JSOT Press, 1990).

K. Elliger, *Das Buch der zwölf Kleinen Propheten* (VTSup, 44; Leiden: Brill, 1992).

R. Haak, *Habakkuk* (VTSup, 44; Leiden: Brill, 1992).

P. Jöcken, *Das Buch Habakuk* (Cologne and Bonn: Peter Hanstein, 1977).

9

THE HISTORY OF
CRITICISM

ALTHOUGH IT WOULD BE impossible here to attempt to narrate
the whole history of criticism of the book of Habakkuk, it is of
the greatest interest that we have a very early commentary
on it in the Dead Sea Scrolls (1QpHab)—the earliest to come
down to us apart from any interpretative process which may
have taken place within the book itself. The Qumran sectaries
interpreted Habakkuk in such a way that it was found to
foretell events of their own time. It is interesting that they see
the 'wicked' as those within Judah whom they identify with
the Hasmonean priests. One of these, described as 'the Wicked
Priest', persecuted the founder of the sect whom they call the
'Teacher of Righteousness'. The latter and his followers are
the 'righteous'. God has raised up the 'Kittim' (Romans)—they
read this word in place of the MT's *kasdîm* (Chaldeans)—
through whom he will punish the Wicked Priest. The complaint of Hab. 1.12-13 means that God will not use foreign
nations to destroy his people. He will rather use the elect
among them to destroy the nations. However, even the wicked
among his people who take warning from the distress caused
by the Kittim and return to keeping the law will be deemed to
have expiated their guilt.

Of course this somewhat breathtaking method of scriptural
exegesis was one that the Qumran sectaries shared with their
contemporaries—many examples of it are found in the New
Testament. Yet it is of interest for two reasons in particular. It
shows that the sectaries were already facing some of the
questions posed above which have exercised commentators of

all times, and it shows how words of Scripture spoken in one historical context could be found to have relevance in another. It is always possible that something of such a reinterpretative process (or 'recontextualization') has gone on within the handing down of the Habakkuk tradition and might be discernible in the present form of the book.

Arguments for the Unity of the Book

Rather than attempt a description of scholarly views in chronological sequence it seems better to trace the main lines of the arguments under general headings. (A much more detailed analysis and comprehensive account of discussion up to 1977 is to be found in Jöcken's work already referred to.)

Arguments for a Unity of Sense in the Book as it Stands
This may be called the 'traditional' approach; it is outlined by A.B. Davidson who, somewhat hesitantly, endorses it. This interpretation reads the complaint of 1.2-4 as referring to internal injustice inflicted by powerful and wicked Judaean leaders against their compatriots. How can God tolerate such conditions? The answer comes in 1.5-11 in which God assures the prophet that he is bringing the Babylonians as an instrument of judgment against the wicked of his own people. This is not predictive, for the Babylonians have clearly been long on the scene. But closer experience of Babylonian military intervention and of conditions under their overlordship raises further difficulties for the prophet. How can God use such people against those who are more righteous than they (1.12-17)? The prophet therefore takes his stand on his watchtower waiting to hear God's answer which, when it comes (2.2-5), assures him that the wicked—that is, the Babylonians—will fail, but that the righteous shall live if they remain faithful. The series of woes in 2.6-20 predicts the fall of the oppressive Babylonians. This is the real issue for Habakkuk, according to Davidson, who leaves open the question whether the psalm in ch. 3 is integral to the book. Clearly it does not conflict with such an interpretation.

There are obvious difficulties in such a view, as Davidson

himself acknowledges. If the Babylonians are being sent by God as a judgment against the wicked among his own people, how can the latter then be described as 'more righteous' than the instrument of divine justice (v. 13); and why does the prophet who in vv. 1-4 longed for judgment against them complain about its severity when it comes? Further, if the ways of the Babylonians are already known (vv. 5-11), why is the prophet so dismayed that he attacks them vehemently in vv. 13-17? Such a change in attitude may not be impossible to imagine when general knowledge of the Babylonians becomes actual first-hand experience, but it remains strange. It was Wellhausen who said,

> In the same moment when the prophet, deeply indignant about the contempt of law within his own people, announces the Chaldeans as the penalty, he could not utter a deeply felt song of complaint about the ill-treatment of his people by the Chaldeans (cited by W.W. Cannon).

Another attempt to find unity in the book as it stands which attempts to face this difficulty is that of W.W. Cannon. He believed that the apparent inconsistencies can be removed if the various sections are seen to have dated from different times. So the first complaint of 1.2-4 with its parallels to Jeremiah dates from the early part of the reign of Jehoiakim (609–598 BCE), while the first divine response of 1.5-11 followed Babylon's victory in the battle of Carchemish in 608. This victory, while it delighted Jeremiah (46.10-12), dismayed Habakkuk who saw what it would mean for Israel. So the prophet renews his complaint (1.12-17) in the light of the truly oppressive nature of the Chaldeans which has now become apparent. This leads to the assurance of the second oracle (2.1-4) which, with its promise of failure for the wicked and life for the righteous, refers to the wicked and faithful within the Jewish community. The woes were anti-Babylonian and followed the deportation of many leading Jews to Babylon in 597 BCE.

A very similar position is taken by J.P. Hyatt, having been anticipated by S.R. Driver, who reflects that 'i. 12ff. may express the perplexity which [Habakkuk] became conscious of afterwards when the character of the Chaldeans became more fully known to him'. However, this, even if the units could be dated in such a way, does not really overcome the problem. It simply means that the prophet came to see somewhat later that his hoped-for deliverers were unacceptable. Such a lack of prevision would not have been likely to commend a Hebrew prophet to his contemporaries and successors. But, in any event, the material itself does not provide enough indications to fix the individual units as precisely in a succession of historical events as Cannon would like. Indeed, a number of commentators have argued that the book may have been kept deliberately vague about historical detail so that it could be found relevant in a number of situations. This is suggested by J.D. Watts, J.H. Eaton and E. Achtemeier, who says that 'both Habakkuk himself and later editors have given the work a universal and timeless validity'. This is a very important observation to which we shall need to return.

Arguments for Unity based on Cultic Function
One of the earliest scholars to argue for an essential unity of the book on the basis of its use in the worship of the community was E. Sellin. In the fifth edition of his *Introduction to the Old Testament* he found a solution to the book's problems by seeing it as a 'prophetic liturgy' in which 1.5-11 was not an announcement of a future event but a description of present distress. He believed that the book was composed by the prophet for a day of prayer by the community when it was labouring under the oppression of the Babylonians (whether this was in the reign of Jehoiakim or Zedekiah was not clear). 1.2-4 was the first lament of the people, to which 1.5-11 was the first oracular answer announcing that God had appointed the Chaldeans as a scourge for the whole world. 1.12-17, remonstrating with God for using such pagans against the upright, was followed by a second oracle (2.1-5) assuring the prophet, and through him the people, that the faithful would live while the godless (that is the Chaldeans) would fall. In response to this the prophet utters his fivefold woe against the Babylonians, and in 3.2-15 reports his powerful vision of Yahweh's victorious battle against his enemies. In 3.16-19 the prophet provides the community with a closing hymn of praise.

In spite of all their present distress their future deliverance is certain. Thus, apart from a few minor glosses, the book is to be seen as a unity. (In earlier editions Sellin had argued for its unity but followed Duhm in dating it in the Greek period.)

Another scholar who argued strongly on similar grounds for the unity of the book was P. Humbert. He saw Habakkuk as a cultic prophet who was influenced by earlier prophecy. He rejected readings of the book which rested on drastic reordering of the text since, he argued, if one doubts the function and integrity of the text as it stands, it becomes impossible to resolve the problems of interpretation. In fact, he claimed, his own careful analysis of the text suggests that there is a 'harmonious structure' to the book in which there is a logical progression from the complaints to the oracles, from the oracles to the curses and from the curses to the final prayer of ch. 3. 1.5 announces a particular act of God in the near future and v. 6 shows that those he is raising are to be his agents in response to the prayer of 1.2-4, and that they are already known. But 1.12-17, like 1.2-4, refers to oppression within Judah by the king, the very person whom Yahweh has appointed to champion the claims of the righteous; and the singular of 2.4 also points to a particular individual best understood as the king, while the woes of 2.6-20 with their close parallels to Jeremiah are also directed against the Judaean king, Jehoiakim. Chapter 3, with its lack of reference to any particular historical foe or situation, may have been a vision that Habakkuk received in the sanctuary while he was carrying out his cultic functions. Thus he presents before God the complaints of the community in their suffering under the unjust rule of Jehoiakim; 1.5-11, 2.1-5 and ch. 3 all bring oracular assurance of God's intention to deliver the righteous among his people.

J. Lindblom also stated quite emphatically that 'the Book of Habakkuk is not the work of a secondary collector of prophetic revelations, but a composition by the prophet himself, who was certainly a cultic prophet at the temple of Jerusalem'. It is similar to Isaiah 24–27, to which Lindblom refers as a 'cantata' used on a specific occasion in Jerusalem. Lindblom finds no inconsistency in seeing in 1.5-11 an allusion to the

Chaldeans after 612 BCE, appointed by Yahweh to chastise his own people. Nevertheless, as a cult prophet, Habakkuk intercedes for his people, 'hoping that through faithful adherence to Yahweh they will save their life'.

Eaton suggested that the whole book may have been prepared for recitation at a public festival, with the psalm of ch. 3 composed 'as its crown'. However, if we compare his conclusions with those of Humbert and Lindblom we can see that this common 'cultic' approach does not result in any uniformity of view about its historical reference, since Eaton is one of those who believes that the 'wicked' are the Assyrians, although the addition of ch. 3 would fit the reign of Josiah when conditions would again have been suitable for praise and celebration. Sweeney, noting that the word *mišmeret* (RSV 'watchtower') in 2.1 appears in 2 Chron. 7.6; 8.14; 35.2 as a technical term for priestly or levitical positions in the performance of the cult, deduced that Habakkuk was a temple prophet. He also found the book to be 'a coherent structural unity' although he supported this view by arguing that the Chaldeans in 1.5-11 are seen not as the divine answer to the prophet's problem of the injustices inflicted on society but as a further example of such injustice. In this he followed a line suggested by M.D. Johnson who urged that the conditions of injustice in 1.2-4 were those inflicted by Judaean rulers operating under Babylonian control, the Babylonians thus being part of the problem of injustice rather than its answer.

One more scholar who takes this view may be mentioned. J. Jeremias believed that Habakkuk was a pre-exilic temple prophet, and that the basic form of the book is that of 'a lament liturgy'. But although 2.1-5 shows that Habakkuk predicted salvation, he was not a salvation prophet in any narrow sense since he proclaimed words of divine judgment against Israel. However, unlike Amos, he did not see the disaster as total, but held out salvation for the righteous. As a 'watchman' over the house of Israel he warns them, but also predicts *šālôm*. Thus he is to be seen as a cult prophet who was influenced by the canonical prophets.

Such views have by no means gone unchallenged. P. Jöcken ('War Habakuk ein Kultprophet?'), for example, maintained that there is no evidence to suggest either that a pre-exilic Habakkuk was a cult prophet or that a later, post-exilic redaction had attempted to present him as one. In *Das Buch Habakuk* he returned to the attack in more detail. While there are cultic forms in the book (1.2-4, 12a and 13 are a 'song of lament, parallel to those found in Jeremiah and some Psalms'), there are also non-cultic, traditional prophetic forms. 1.5-11, for example, is a threat of judgment rather than a 'salvation oracle' and, as such, parallel to other similar material in the prophets. Indeed, announcing judgment against their own people does not seem to have been part of the function of cultic prophets. Even 2.1-3 need not have been set in the temple but may express a more general view of the prophet as one who 'watches' over his people. 2.4-5 deals with the question of theodicy in a broader way than if it were merely a cultic oracle; it has parallels in other prophets, for instance Ezek. 18.9 and Isa. 7.9, and indeed elsewhere, for instance Gen. 15.6, Lev. 25.18, 26.3ff. Again, the woe oracles of 2.6b-19 represent a general prophetic form with no special cultic connections, while even the psalm in ch. 3, which could have been taken from a liturgical songbook, is now set in the framework of a prophetic form. Thus, for Jöcken, Habakkuk was a prophet of judgment, like Ezekiel, although Jöcken also believes, as we shall see later, that his words were given an anti-Babylonian thrust in a late exilic redaction.

Jöcken has a case in his treatment of the individual units, and, without prejudging the issue at this point, it may be admitted that we possess no satisfactory comparative material which would enable us to justify the existence of such a cultic form as has been postulated, and so to make this an argument to defend the essential unity of the book. Other alleged examples of 'prophetic liturgies', such as Hosea 14, or even the book of Joel (see below), do not correspond with any exactness to the book of Habakkuk. Moreover, the variety of theories offered by the proponents of a cultic interpretation of historical contexts and cultic events which might have fitted such a liturgy does not inspire confidence in the method. This is not to say that cultic prophets did not use laments or bring answering oracles, nor that such forms have played no part in the shaping of the book.

Arguments for Unity based on Form-Critical Grounds
A number of scholars who have not felt able to be quite as specific about the cultic role of Habakkuk as those considered above have, nevertheless, believed that the present form of the book shows the influence of cultic forms. They have tended in the main to argue for an essential unity but on the basis of form-critical considerations. So G. Horst, while he does not believe that the oracles have necessarily been arranged in chronological order (so that 1.5-11 might have been the latest passage to be introduced) thinks that they are nevertheless linked in a liturgical pattern of lament and divine answer. Direct cultic use is unlikely since the book could only with difficulty be described as a 'liturgy'. Nevertheless the liturgical arrangement may have been intended for lectionary use.

W.H. Brownlee argued that the 'liturgical character of Habakkuk's prophecy as understood in recent years eliminates the necessity of rearrangements of the text (which were once so prevalent in criticism of the Book of Habakkuk)'. He saw the first lament (1.1-4) as pointing to non-observance of the law within Judah. Such laxity would be an effect of foreign domination. The first oracle (1.5-11) is addressed to the lapsed in Judaean society against whom the Chaldeans will be Yahweh's instrument of wrath. The second lament (1.12-17) concerns the character of the Chaldeans and so questions the character of Yahweh who uses them. 'There is no reason why the prophet should coin a different ethical vocabulary for the sinful Chaldeans than for the apostate Judeans'. The second oracle, which is given only after an agonizing wait, is 'a message of faith in the Lord of History who will give final victory to the faithful righteous'; that is, the faithful within Judah, not Judah as a whole. The singers of the taunt songs of 2.5b-17 are 'the nations who have borne the brunt of the conqueror'. As for the psalm of ch. 3, Brownlee contends that 'The present study reinforces the probability of its composition by Habakkuk', for it parallels the cultic nature of Habakkuk's laments and oracles and the taunt song of the nations. Thus, for Brownlee, the form of the book suggests a coherent unity, even though he believes that there was an exilic redaction which redirected the prophet's original words about Assyria to Babylon. The parallels between such later additions (2.14, 15-16, 18-19) and Second Isaiah suggest a strong theological affinity between the groups who so redacted the book and the disciples of Second Isaiah.

The strongest statement of the case for unity on form-critical grounds is that of R.D. Haak. He rejects the many attempts to rearrange the text and even to find later, exilic additions which have changed the thrust of the book: 'The form-critical study and translation of the text developed above would indicate that these approaches are not necessary'. Haak bases his approach on the form-critical study of the 'psalm of lament' initiated by Gunkel and elaborated by Mowinckel. He points out (rightly) that recent scholars have questioned Gunkel's rigid demarcation of the 'individual' and 'communal' laments in that the individual speaker may often be a repre-sentative of a wider group—a prophet or, more especially, a king. He then turns to Koch's analysis of the individual complaint in which he finds the following components: (1) invocation to God; (2) petition; (3) lament (or complaint); (4) grounds for deliverance or expression of trust; (5) protesta-tions of innocence; (6) certainty of a hearing; (7) an oracle of salvation which itself divides into introduction, assurance of help, result of divine intervention and statement of relation between God and the supplicant; (8) hymnic elements.

Haak finds these elements in Habakkuk in a double com-plaint. 1.1-4 consists of invocation and complaint: 1.5-6 is an oracle of salvation; 1.7-11 is an expression of certainty and 1.12 a hymnic element. The cycle begins again with 1.13–2.1, which sets out grounds for deliverance, complaint and petition. Haak sees the object of the two complaints as the same:

> They may, in fact, refer to the same general historical situation. The complaint form is not a chronological account within itself. There is no formal reason why a single complaint may not have multiple sections, use a variety of images, and even have an oracle of salvation intervening.

He cites Psalm 60 and Jer. 11.18–12.6 as examples of this arrangement. The second complaint is then followed by an oracle of salvation (2.2-4) and an expression of certainty (2.5-20). Haak admits that 'woe cries' are not not normally associated with complaints, but here they 'are used as an expansion of the complaint form, specifically the part of the complaint which is an expression of certainty'. Further, they express the 'reversal of fortune' theme which is familiar in the complaints. Perhaps this is why the junction between the complaint and the woes in 2.5 is not clear. Chapter 3 is a hymn, but one which is patterned after those that occur in the psalms of lament; that is why the hymnic element is followed by a lament in 3.16-17. This culminates, however, in an expression of certainty (vv. 18-19).

Haak makes an important point when he says that such a form-critical approach should make one cautious about looking for detailed and consistent historical situations, since some elements owe more to their traditional form, and act less as bearers of historical weight. Such consistency of form-critical features throughout the book makes some cultic connection 'quite probable', although it is difficult to distinguish between an actual liturgy and the imitation of a liturgical form. Haak believes that Habakkuk's complaints are not merely personal but reflect the breakdown of law and order in society. The use of the singular terms 'the wicked' and 'the just', the references to 'ruling' (1.14) and 'war' (1.15-17) and the allusions to the breakdown of law and justice within the community all suggest a historical context in which a just king has been supplanted in Judah by an evil one. Parallels with Jeremiah's attacks on Jehoiakim suggest that he must have been the wicked king in whose place the Egyptians appointed the pro-Babylonian Jehoahaz; that is why Habakkuk sees the coming of the Babylonians as Yahweh's answer to the wicked reign of Jehoiakim. One conclusion from all this is that the book is 'a unified composition in the period of 605–603 BCE'.

Here again we see the strength of arguments which find a clear reflection of cultic forms in the book of Habakkuk, such as the psalm of lament in which a prophet presents the people's complaints to God on their behalf and brings an answering oracle from God. However, some of the alleged parallels are overdrawn. It seems unlikely that any critic would read 1.7-11 as 'an expression of certainty' without a predisposition to do so on other grounds. It is true that the various elements in the psalms of lament often appear in a strange order and that some elements are often missing altogether. Haak cites Psalm 60 as an example of an answering oracle's being followed as well as preceded by complaint. He might have added, however, that this is virtually the only example of a psalm of lament in the Psalter in which we find such an oracle at all. In general the oracular elements appear in other types of psalms; but in the lament psalms in which we find a dramatic switch of mood from one of despair to one of confidence the oracle is lacking (see Day, *The Psalms*). Further, it is a pity that Haak did not pay heed to his own warning that in such psalms the presence of traditional elements may well mean that we cannot find detailed historical contexts for them. If Habakkuk were really a prophet in the way Haak suggests, and if the book should be seen as conforming to the pattern of the psalms of lament, a detailed historical application is the last thing that we should expect to have survived. Echoes of Jehoiakim there may be (see below); but Haak's detailed historical analysis depends upon a literal reading of psalm-like material in which metaphor and symbol tend to predominate over literalism and explicit historical allusion.

Arguments against the Unity of the Book

Where there is such a welter of conflicting critical opinions about the book of Habakkuk it is often difficult to label different points of view systematically. For example, we have noted that Brownlee sees the book as essentially a unity as it stands, but leaves open the question as to whether it has arrived in that form as a result of a complex redactional process. Some of those whose views I will now examine do not differ very markedly from that position, but all of them assume, in one way or another, that the book was not created as a unity but has had unity thrust upon it.

K. Budde attempted to meet the problem of God's punishment of one set of evil-doers (leading Judaeans) by means of another, even more evil power (the Babylonians), by saying that the complaints were directed against the cruelty and oppression of the Assyrians. It was to deliver his people from the Assyrians' power that God was raising up the Babylonians. To meet the problem that this announcement (in 1.5-11) is then followed by a second complaint (1.12-17), Budde suggested that 1.5-11 was originally placed after 2.4, and thus served as a confirmation of the assurance Habakkuk had received that 'the just would live by his faithfulness'. Presumably, then, the present order of the book must be the result of Judah's later bitter experience at the hand of the Babylonians when the 'deliverers' turned out to be their destroyers. (Wellhausen had claimed that 1.5-11 was from a different hand altogether, as had Nowack.) A. Weiser agreed with Budde that the Assyrians had been the object of the complaints, but believed that it was a mistake to think that the units must have been arranged chronologically. The complaints and oracles may, rather, have been individual units arising from the same general background, but reflecting the prophet's varying reactions as he waited for the judgment he had announced to appear. The present arrangement, Weiser thought, probably owes a good deal to the use of the material by the congregation in worship.

Others found different historical allusions here. Elliger, for example, thought that the wicked whose oppression was the theme of the complaints were the Egyptians, from whom the Babylonians were seen as the divinely sent deliverers. Habakkuk must, therefore, be dated between 609 and 598—that is, between the death of Josiah when Judah passed under Egyptian control and the first deportation of Judaeans by the Babylonians. Elliger thought that the prophet himself gave the book its present general (liturgical) shape, but allowed that later redaction may have given it an anti-Babylonian thrust.

The obvious objection to such arguments is that no reference to the Assyrians or the Egyptians (and certainly not to Duhm's Greeks; see below) remains in the text as we have it. Yet it is supposedly on the basis of the text as we have it that

such arguments are constructed. This is always the weakness
of redaction-critical theories (see above). In any event, hope in
the Babylonians as deliverers would have been short-lived;
and, since in 1.5-11 their character is already well known, it is
strange that they should have been so thought of. And if they
had been so thought of, what effect would this be likely to
have on the credibility of the prophet who made such an
announcement in the first place?

Several scholars have posited a complex redactional process
behind the present form of the book. E. Otto (in 'Die Theologie
des Buches Habakuk') believed that Habakkuk himself
preached a message very similar to that of Jeremiah. In his
laments, oracles and woe-cries he attacked evils prevalent
within Judaean society itself. So in 1.2-4, 12a, 13-14 we hear
his laments against such evils, and to this Yahweh responds
with an oracle (2.1-5abα) assuring the prophet that evil-doers
will not survive; so the woe-cries of 2.6b, 7, 9, 10abβ, 12, 11,
15, 16 are the prophet's laments over them as though they
were already dead. To this Habakkuk tradition, however, 1.5-
11 and 12b were added to give the prophet's complaints about
evil-doers within Judah an anti-Babylonian thrust; and so it
was at this stage that the present structure of a double lament
and oracle was shaped.

The second lament of 1.15-17, according to Otto, was also
given an anti-Babylonian meaning at this stage, the work of
a redactor whose hand is also seen in 2.5bβ, 6a, 8, 10bα, 13,
14 and 17. This was then set in an early post-exilic framework
by the addition of 1.1, 2.18-20 and a first form of 3.3-15 and
16. A final stage put the psalm in ch. 3 to cultic use by the
addition of 3.1, 3, 9, 13, 17-19. This whole process took place
between 612 BCE and the early post-exilic period, a period of
less than one hundred years. Much earlier Rothstein had
argued that the oppressor criticized by the prophet was King
Jehoiakim together with his supporters. Thus the prophet was
active after the battle of Carchemish, when the Babylonians
had appeared on the scene, but before they had come against
Judah. Habakkuk therefore saw the Babylonians as divinely
appointed deliverers. However, an exilic redactor had resolved
the tension by redirecting Habakkuk's oracles *against* the

Babylonians, showing them in a much more critical light. Jöcken also believes that it is necessary to distinguish the original message of Habakkuk from later redaction. He finds the original message in 1.2-4, 12a, 13; 2.1-3 and 1.5-11 (in that order). These verses show that Habakkuk was not a cult prophet but that he attacked the sins of the community in the manner of other post-exilic prophets. As an announcement by God, 1.5-11 was also to be seen as a threat of judgment, the Babylonians being the instrument God would use against his own people. However, a late exilic redaction (to be found in 1.11b, 12b, 14-17; 2.5bγδ, 8, 10bα, 13b, 17b, 18, 19b; 3.2-16, 18-19) gave the whole message an anti-Babylonian thrust.

A recent commentator who also traces a complex redaction history in the book is K. Seybold. As it stands the book is in two parts (chs. 1–2 and ch. 3), each with its own super-scription. Neither part is a literary unity. The first part has been formed out of laments in the first-person speech of the prophet in 1.2ff. and 1.12ff., a divine response in 1.5ff. and a visionary scene in 2.1ff. But the abrupt change of speakers and alternation between the singular and plural (in 1.5, 12, 14; 2.1 and 6) make this difficult to elucidate. How do the laments and the oracles fit together? If 1.5-11 speaks of a Babylonian invasion ordained by God, to which power do the woes of ch. 2 relate? Seybold cites with approval H. Schmidt's attempt to isolate all the 'psalm-like' passages of the book (apart from ch. 3) which he found to exhibit a marked unity. He believes that these sections are of independent origin but found their way into the text from the margin of an old scroll. Seybold identifies such material in 1.2-4, 12-13; 2.1, 4, 20 and 3.7, 8, 13b-14, 17-19. These represent the laments and thanksgivings of one who has been accused but pronounced innocent and, like ch. 3, originally had nothing whatever to do with the book. The original prophetic oracle material is therefore to be found in 1.5-11, 14-17; 2.1-3 and 5-19. These passages reveal a prophet who spoke against injustice within Judah and who saw such a society as little able to prepare for the dangers which would come upon it from outside. Originally the enemy whose advance is predicted may have been either the Scythians or the Medes. Similarities to the oracles of the young Jeremiah (Jer. 2–6) suggest a time in the Assyrian period of domination, perhaps about 630 BCE. The woes of ch. 2 are akin to prophetic curses and are parallel to similar forms found in Amos, Isaiah and Nahum. The direction of the woe cries and the oracle of 1.5-11 against the Babylonians represent a late exilic redaction, perhaps occurring about 550 BCE. At this time the Persians were on the march, and the prophet's vision in which he is told to wait for God's deliverance is understood to be finding fulfilment in the Persian assault against Babylon in much the same way as Second Isaiah saw this. Chapter 3, drawing as it does on old theophany hymns, reflects just such an outlook, and was added at this time. The psalm-like material which draws on the prayer of the accused and thus raises the question of divine justice was added by a later, post-exilic redactor who wanted to call for trust from his contemporaries at a time when for them too God's ways seemed difficult to fathom. It would fit well a period about 400 BCE.

In addition to the objections to such redaction-critical approaches mentioned above, it should be said that there is a considerable element of subjectivity involved. There is a risk of circular argument if redactional layers are isolated only or primarily on the basis of a prior conviction as to what can and cannot be original to the prophet. There clearly are tensions within the text which require explanation; but we may find after redaction-critical analysis that it is difficult to interpret the text at all, if it appears as the result of such a complex process that no consistent voice can be discerned. We should examine other avenues of analysis before accepting such a negative conclusion.

Further Reading

E. Achtemeier, *Nahum–Malachi* (Interpretation; Atlanta: John Knox, 1986).

M.H. Brownlee, 'The Composition of Habakkuk', in A. Caquot and M. Philonenko (eds.), *Hommages à André Dupont-Sommer* (Paris: Maisonneuve, 1971), pp. 255-75.

W.W. Cannon, 'The Integrity of Habakkuk 1–2', *ZAW* 43 (1925), pp. 62-90.

A.B. Davidson, *Nahum, Habakkuk and Zephaniah* (CBS; Cambridge: Cambridge University Press, 1896).

S.R. Driver, *The Minor Prophets*, II (CB: Edinburgh: Nelson, 1906).

Eaton, *Obadiah, Nahum, Habakkuk, Zephaniah*.

G. Horst, *Die Zwölf Kleinen Propheten* (HAT, 14; Tübingen: Mohr [Paul Siebeck], 1964).

P. Humbert, *Problèmes du livre d'Habacuc* (Neuchatel: Delachâux & Niestlé, 1944).

H.P. Hyatt, 'Habakkuk', *PCB*, pp. 637-39.

J. Jeremias, *Kultprophetie und Gerichtsverkündigung in der späten Königszeit Israels* (WMANT, 35, 1970), pp. 55-110.

P. Jöcken, 'War Habakuk ein Kultprophet?', in H.J. Fabry (ed.), *Bausteine biblischer Theologie (Festschrift für G.J. Botterweck)* (Cologne and Bonn: Peter Hanstein, 1977), pp. 319-32.

—*Das Buch Habakuk* (Cologne and Bonn: Peter Hanstein, 1977).

M.D. Johnson, 'The Paralysis of Torah in Habakkuk 1:4', *VT* 35 (1985), pp. 257-66.

K. Koch, *The Growth of the Biblical Tradition* (trans. S.M. Cupitt; New York: A. & C. Black, 1969).

J. Lindblom, *Prophecy in Ancient Israel* (Oxford: Basil Blackwell, 1962).

E. Otto, 'Die Stellung der Wehe-Worte in der Verkündigung des Propheten Habakuk', *ZAW* 89 (1977), pp. 73-107.

—'Die Theologie des Buches Habakuk', *VT* 35 (1985), pp. 274-95.

J.W. Rothstein, 'Über Habakuk Kap. 1 u. 2', *TSK* 67 (1894), pp. 51-85.

E. Sellin, *Einleitung in das Alte Testament* (Leipzig: Quelle & Meyer, 5th edn, 1929).

H. Schmidt, 'Ein Psalm in Buche Habakuk', *ZAW* 62 (1950), pp. 52-63.

Seybold, *Nahum, Habakuk, Zephanja*.

M.A. Sweeney, 'Structure, Genre and Intent in the Book of Habakkuk', *VT* 41 (1991), pp. 63-83.

J.D. Watts, *The Books of Joel, Obadiah, Jonah, Nahum, Habakkuk and Zephaniah* (CBC; Cambridge: Cambridge University Press, 1975).

10

THE PROPHET
AND HIS TIMES

FROM OUR SURVEY OF critical opinion about the book it will be
seen that the attempt to locate Habakkuk in his historical context depends to a great extent on our answer to other
questions. We know no details of Habakkuk's life. His name
has been linked (by Noth) to an Akkadian plant name, but
that is scarcely informative. In the Septuagint the story of Bel
and the Dragon (an addition to the book of Daniel) speaks of
'the prophet Habakkuk', who is described as 'the son of
Joshua of the tribe of Levi'. His part in this narrative is
somewhat fanciful. While Daniel is languishing in a den of
lions in Babylon, Habakkuk in Judah is taking a meal out to
harvesters in the field; but God tells him to take it instead to
Daniel in the lions' den in Babylon. Not unreasonably,
Habakkuk says that he does not know where either Babylon
or the lions' den is, whereupon the angel of the Lord lifts him
by the hair of his head and carries him there, together with
the food. The only crumb that we might glean from such a
tale is that tradition appeared to remember Habakkuk as a
priest; this might have something to say about his possible
role as a cultic or temple prophet. But it is a lean meal of
information for us.

In the absence of any textual evidence to suggest that the
name is secondary, we may take the reference to the
'Chaldeans' in 1.6 as literal (while recognizing that in the
course of time it might come to be read as stereotypic, repre-
senting other great powers who, in their turn, threatened the
people of God). Since their military methods and ferocity seem

to be known, it is reasonable to suppose that this oracle at least originated in the period of neo-Babylonian imperial expansion, which really began with the reign of Nabopolassar (626–605. For the general historical background of the period see above). If the injustice complained of in 1.2-4 and 12-17 did, as some have argued, refer to oppression under the Assyrians, and if the Babylonians are seen as the divine answer to the cries of the prophet, somewhere about 612 BCE would be an appropriate date, depending on whether 1.5-11 is a prediction of a deliverance yet to come or descriptive of one which has already taken place, for it was in that year that Nineveh, the Assyrian capital, fell. On the other hand, if the oppressors complained of were the Egyptians, as others have urged, then the period of 609–605 would seem more appropriate.

It must be admitted that there is little compelling evidence for either of these dates. This is well illustrated by the recollection that Duhm interpreted the same material (he read the word *Kittim* in 1.6 in place of the Hebrew *Chasdim*) as referring to 'the Greeks', seeing the coming deliverer as Alexander the Great (to support this view he emended the difficult Hebrew text of the second line of 1.9 to read 'From Gomer their direction is eastward'). Few would now find such cavalier treatment of the text acceptable, but it shows how susceptible the material is to varying historical interpretations.

Some have felt enough confidence to make very precise historical judgments on the matter. E. Nielsen took the singular form of the words 'righteous' and 'wicked' in 1.4 and 13 to refer to specific individuals, and saw the whole complaint as referring to the deportation of Jehoahaz (called Shallum in Jer. 22.10-12 where the prophet is called to 'weep for him who goes away') and his replacement by the wicked Jehoiakim. Habakkuk would thus refer to the events of 609–608 BCE. This argument has also received detailed reworking more recently by R.D. Haak. Rothstein found close parallels between Jeremiah's complaints against King Jehoiakim (Jer. 22.13-19) and Habakkuk's description of the oppression of 'the wicked', and saw here a reference to the disorders and injustice of Jehoiakim's reign (even though he allowed for some, later, anti-Babylonian additions). Humbert saw all the complaints in the book as being made against injustice and oppression within Judah, and saw Jehoiakim as the tyrant. Jöcken agreed with Humbert that the original message of Habakkuk was directed against Judaean oppression, but differed from him in finding unmistakable allusions in the present form of the book to a foreign oppressor. These passages (1.14, 17; 2.5b, 8, 10bα, 13-14, 17b; 3.12, 13a, 15) he attributed to a later, exilic, anti-Babylonian redaction.

In fact the references to injustice in 1.2-4 are quite general; they complain of a breakdown in law and order. M.D. Johnson argued that 1.4 speaks of a 'paralysis' of Torah. He pointed out that such conditions may have been due to the damaging effects of foreign domination, under which the proper maintenance by native leaders of Yahweh's will for his people became impossible. Johnson believed that Habakkuk was 'a disillusioned Deuteronomist'—that is, one who had hoped for much from Josiah's religious reform, but who now saw its effects nullified because of foreign control. Johnson also found consistency in the complaints by stressing that the Babylonians are seen by the prophet as part of the problem, not as the divine answer to it. In fact it is difficult to attempt to date Habakkuk by any very specific reference to Josiah's reforms (621 BCE). We do not know how far the Deuteronomistic historians have exaggerated and systemized their account of their extent and effects, how universal they were in their application or how far Josiah's failure and early death may have led to their widespread abandonment. The latter state of affairs is certainly suggested by the bitter attacks by Jeremiah and Ezekiel on the religious abuses and social malpractices of their contemporaries.

1.12-17 is as general as 1.2-4. It could refer specifically to the Chaldeans of 1.5-11 but also, as Humbert and others have argued, to an oppressive Judaean ruler. The indictments in the woes in ch. 2 often recall Jeremiah's attacks on King Jehoiakim; yet, again, the language used is general and figurative enough to be applicable at several levels. It does appear that we must take seriously the views of those who have suggested that the historical references in the book are deliberately vague and general (see above). We must content ourselves at present with the rather indefinite conclusion that a date in the last part of the seventh century, which puts Habakkuk in the time of the spread of the Babylonians throughout the ancient Near East and sees him as a contemporary of Jeremiah, with whom he shared a very similar point of view, would be quite appropriate.

Further Reading

B. Duhm, *Das Buch Habakuk* (Tübingen: Mohr, 1906).

M. Noth, *Die israelitischen Personennamen* (BWANT, 3.10; Stuttgart: Kohlhammer, 1928).

E. Nielsen, 'The Righteous and the Wicked in Habaqquq', *Studia Theologica* 6 (1953), pp. 54-78.

11

THE THEOLOGY AND
FUNCTION OF THE BOOK

THE OPENING LAMENT is spoken by the prophet in the first person directly addressing Yahweh. The formula 'How long?' (Heb. *'ad 'ānāh*) is a familiar one occurring in psalms of lament, both individual and communal, along with the synonymous but more frequent *'ad māthai*. It can occur in speech between human beings, often expressing impatience, as in Jos. 18.3; Job 8.2; 18.2; 19.2) and it can also express God's impatience with human beings (Exod. 16.28; Num. 14.11). Its liturgical use is found in psalms of lament such as Ps. 13.1-2 (Heb. 2-3) asking how long God will forget the psalmist and conceal himself, and Ps. 62.3 (Heb. 4), where the sufferer asks how long his enemies will persecute him. The latter psalm is of particular interest since it appears to contain an oracular answer from God to the psalmist: 'Once God has spoken this; twice have I heard this: that power belongs to God' (Ps. 62.11 [Heb. 12]). The cry *'ad māthai* is found in other psalms of lament (Pss. 6.3 [Heb. 4]; 74.10; 80.4 [Heb. 5]; 90.13; 94.3).

In Habakkuk, the complaint is that God appears to be doing nothing about violence, iniquity, trouble, destruction, the 'paralysis of Torah' (Johnson) or the oppression of the 'righteous' (or 'innocent' as the word may often be rendered), while justice is administered only in a twisted way. All of these terms are fairly general. The singular form of 'wicked' and 'righteous' in v. 4 might suggest that the prophet had particular individuals in mind, but it need not do so. The verse is far more likely to bear a general sense here—*all* the righteous are beset by the many wicked. It is true that the responsibility

for establishing justice rested primarily with the king; but, as
with Amos and other prophets, failure here can be a charge
levelled against the governing classes in general (cf. Amos
5.15, where the plural imperatives show that a whole group is
being addressed; cf. also Isa. 5.7). Some have argued that the
reference to the breach of Torah suggests an inner-Judaean
situation, but it is by no means impossible that foreigners also
could be seen as breaking God's law (compare the opening
oracles against the nations in the book of Amos); and, as some
have suggested, it was often when under foreign domination
that native leaders were either careless or impotent with regard
to their responsibility to establish 'justice' in society. In fact
this passage, which is clearly structured in the cultic form of
the lament, employs, like the laments, very general language.
In this way the laments lent themselves to use in a variety of
circumstances and situations (cf. Johnson; Day, *The Psalms*).
What is clear is that this passage expresses the same indignation at the suffering of the victims of injustice and oppression
as is found in all the major pre-exilic prophets as well as in the
psalms. (For the many parallels between the teaching of the
pre-exilic prophets and the psalms see Eaton.)

It should be clear from our survey of criticism of the book
that it is the divine oracle in 1.5-11 that has occasioned so
many difficulties for exegetes. Verse 6 makes it clear that this
is first-person speech of Yahweh, even though the Hebrew of
v. 5, which lacks a personal subject, theoretically leaves a little
room for doubt. The oracle describes the fierceness, self-
confidence and dread military prowess of those who impose
their own kind of 'justice' on those whom they conquer. They
are invincible. The only hint of condemnation comes in v. 11,
where the text is difficult. It probably means either that they
ascribe their strength to their own god or that they make a
'god' of their strength ('guilty' in the RSV [v. 11] is an improbable rendering).

By far the most surprising aspect of this 'oracle', however, is
that nothing is said of the purpose for which God has raised
up these 'Chaldeans'. This is most unusual if in fact this is
meant to be, as so many have taken it to be, a divine answer
to the prophet's lament about God's delay in confronting the

injustice which is rampant. In Isaiah 10, where God says that
he is bringing Assyria, it is explicitly stated that this is to
punish his wayward people in Judah. The warnings of a 'foe
from the north' in the early oracles of Jeremiah make it clear
that God is bringing it as an instrument of judgment on his
own people (Jer. 1.13-16; 5.14-15; 6.1-8, 22-26). Even when
Second Isaiah states that God has raised up Cyrus and led
him on his victorious campaigns it is stated that this is in
order that he might fulfil God's purposes, that is, salvation for
his people (Isa. 44.24–45.13). It does seem possible, therefore,
that Johnson was right in saying that this passage is not
intended as the divine answer to the prophet's complaint. The
terrible march of the Babylonians is yet another mystery to
the prophet, the more so since such national movements were
traditionally assigned by Israel's prophets to God's controlling
hand. It is indeed strange that this notion of mystery should
be found in an oracle of Yahweh, but the device does express
forcefully the idea that the apparent answers of Yahweh are
part of the prophet's problem. Injustice at home, injustice in
the international sphere; these are all part of his complaint.
Such a reading does have the advantage of removing the
problem of why the prophet should utter a second complaint
about the very people whom God has apparently called forth
as his answer to his people's need.

1.12-17 is another lament by the prophet. Here also the
theme is the apparent divine indifference to the injustice and
oppression of the very people who have been set by God as
guardians of justice. Again, the Hebrew refers to the oppressor
in the singular, but the same arguments about this must apply
as those mentioned above with regard to the first lament.
Those who have been appointed to establish justice and to
correct those who abuse it are themselves guilty of oppression
of the innocent. Again, the imagery used might be thought
more naturally to apply to a foreign invader, but no doubt
native rulers also made themselves rich at the expense of their
people (cf. the bitter attack on the institution of monarchy in
1 Sam. 8.10-18). It is true that the reference to 'slaying nations'
in v. 17 suggests a foreign imperialist, although there were
many times in the history of the Judaean monarchy when

foreign peoples were unjustly treated (for example David's treatment of the Moabites [2 Sam. 8.2] and of the Edomites [2 Sam. 8.13]). Again, there is just enough ambiguity to permit this passage to be applied to a number of situations, while it breathes the same concern for the rights of the innocent and the oppressed as do the first lament and the divine oracle of 1.5-11 with its horror of the Babylonians.

2.1-5 describes in the first-person speech of the prophet the experience of a vision in which he receives an oracle from Yahweh answering his complaints of ch. 1. The form is not unknown elsewhere in the Old Testament. In Isa. 21.6-10 the prophet is told by Yahweh to set a watchman on a watchtower (clearly, from the context, the prophet himself) who is to look out for the first signs of Yahweh's deliverance of his people from the power of Babylon. The description concludes with the prophet's address to his fellow Judaeans: 'What I have heard from the LORD of hosts, the God of Israel, I announce to you'. In an accompanying oracle the watchman is asked 'What of the night?', to which he replies: 'Morning comes, and also the night. If you will inquire, inquire; come back again'.

I have suggested elsewhere that this idea of the prophet watching through the night of distress for the first signs of God's deliverance which, traditionally, came with the 'morning' has inspired the form of Zechariah's oracles presented in a series of 'visions of the night'. More immediately for our interest here, there are a number of places in the Psalter where a prophet introduces an oracle by a first-person description of a revelation which has come to him. In Psalm 60, a psalm of communal lament, the psalmist introduces a divine, first-person speech oracle giving assurance of victory with the words, 'God has spoken in his sanctuary' (v. 6 [8]). In Psalm 62 the psalmist who has introduced his prayer with the words 'For God alone my soul waits in silence' (1 [2], 5 [6]) says in v. 11 (12): 'Once God has spoken; twice I have heard this: that power belongs to God'. In another psalm of communal lament (Ps. 85) the psalmist says, 'let me hear what God the LORD will speak, for he will speak peace (*šālôm*) to his people' (v. 8 [9]).

Habakkuk also takes his stand on the watchtower and watches 'to see what he will speak to me' (v. 1). The divine oracle in first-person speech which comes to him commands him to wait for the vision, that is, presumably for its fulfilment, since its content is given to him at the time and he is also commanded to write it for all to read (cf. Isa. 30.8). There has been much discussion over the precise meaning and extent of the oracle which is to be written, but its general meaning is clear. It is an oracle of assurance. It announces the ultimate vindication by God of those who trust in him, whatever present appearances there may be to the contrary; and, as such, it fits exactly the pattern of similar oracles in the psalms mentioned above and in Isaiah 21. Vindication of the 'upright' and the 'just' (or 'innocent') also implies judgment of the arrogant oppressor (v. 5). The discussion over the exact meaning and extent of the oracle may be followed, not only in the major commentaries, but also in Brownlee, J.M. Holt, P.J. Southwell, van der Woude, Emerton, J.G. Janzen, J.M. Scott and Gunneweg. It is not possible here to follow all attempts to deal with the difficulties of text and language, but perhaps Emerton's rendering gets as close as any:

> Behold, he whose personality within him is not upright will fly away [i.e. 'perish']; but the righteous man will live because of his faithfulness and the proud man will not be successful.

This understands v. 5b to belong to the woes which follow. Read in this way the divine oracle expresses the same sympathetic point of view for the 'righteous' and the 'upright' against all oppression and exploitation as that found in ch. 1. There is no confession of sin; but this is also lacking in many of the psalms of lament cited above. They champion the cause of those who are being subjected to injustice, and invoke and announce God's intervention on their behalf. They are thus also statements of faith in the justice and power of God. The vision oracle of 2.1-5 clearly belongs to the same category as the psalms of lament. It is therefore best seen as belonging to the temple and the worship of the people, and as reflecting the work of the 'temple' or 'cult' prophets. Nevertheless, there are here many echoes of the pre-exilic prophets' concern for justice, and Keller is right to speak of Habakkuk's 'humanism' and perhaps also to point out parallels with Israel's wisdom traditions (cf. Gunneweg, who links Habakkuk's idea of the suffering righteous with Job 4.12-17). Nevertheless, as many have seen, the most striking parallels are with prophecy; and the famous quotation of 2.4b must be understood in comparison with Ezek. 33.10-16. The real context of Habakkuk is the cult.

The series of five woes which follows also conforms to a familiar kind of prophetic speech. Westermann describes the woe oracle as a frequently occurring variant of the prophetic judgment speech, usually appearing in a series, and says that here particularly we catch echoes of a probably older form: the curse. The normal pattern which he finds in these oracles consists of an announcement followed by the accusation, which has a consistent, stable form. The word *hôy* ('woe') 'introduces a participial sentence that addresses the woe to the one doing evil'. We might add that sometimes the announcement of woe stands alone as a sufficient threat in itself. Often, however, explicit threat is added (cf. Amos 6.4-7), although this may be omitted (cf. Isa. 5.18-23). Even here, however, the woes have been placed in a larger context in which judgment is made explicit (5.24-30). In other cases the accusation may be said to be implicit, as in Amos 6.1-3, where the invitation to those addressed to go and see what happened to Calneh, Hamath and Gath is not intended to be encouraging.

It is important to note that the series of woes in Habakkuk 2 follows this general pattern, because the recognition of a conscious, formal structure and genre may deliver us from a too literalistic and pedantic attempt to identify which historical nation or figure is being referred to. Again we have here the same intermingling of characteristics of a foreign oppressor and of unjust native leaders which we met in the laments of ch. 1. Furthermore, the introduction of the series in v. 6 with the words 'Shall not all these raise up against *him* a proverb, a satirical riddle?' (where the 'him' must refer back to the 'wicked' and 'arrogant' of 2.1-5) suggests that the woes are meant to apply similarly to the wicked generally. We have seen that in the larger prophetic writings in the Old Testament even a specified enemy seems sometimes to be presented as a 'type' or example of a particular sinful attitude. The first woe (6b-8) certainly suggested a foreign power with its reference to 'plundering many nations', yet the sins are exactly those of unjust exploitation of the poor of which further examples occur in the second (9-11), third (12-13) and fourth (15-17) woes, all of which could just as easily refer to native leaders. Indeed, as many have pointed out, there are strong parallels to be found, especially in vv. 9-10, with Jer. 22.13-17, with its clear allusion to the Judaean king Jehoiakim. Yet there are parallels with other prophetic passages in these woes; for example, v. 13 with Jer. 51.58; v. 9 with Obad. v. 3; v. 12 with Mic. 3.10 and Nah. 3.1; vv. 15-16 with Isa. 28.7, 8 and Jer. 25.15-17. This is not to say that in any of these instances one source is 'quoting' another, still less to say which way any dependence may be operating. But it does suggest that we are dealing with general prophetic ideas, language and imagery and, perhaps, should read the text in this way here. For, while the very similar material in Jeremiah 22–23 explicitly refers to Jehoiakim, the fact is that there is no such identification in the woes of Habakkuk 2. Even the last woe in 2.18-19, which is probably an addition, with its change of form and its attack on idolatry in language reminiscent of Second Isaiah shows that the material could be read at some point as a general attack on all forms of sin, of which idolatry was seen as yet another instance. The further addition of v. 20, with its cultic call for 'silence' before the presence of Yahweh in his temple (cf. Zeph. 1.7, Zech. 2.13 [17]) suggests that this is the general stock of temple, or cultic, prophecy. The woes denounce exactly the same forms of evil, foreign and native, as do the laments of ch. 1, revealing the same concern for the weak, the oppressed and the downtrodden, the same passionate concern for the establishment of divine 'justice'.

Yet these woes do more than express such a viewpoint. They do more than make the oppressed the subject of prayer and complaint to Yahweh. They express a prophetic announcement of Yahweh's determination to establish justice by bringing the evil of the wicked on their own heads and inverting the present orders of power. The woe or curse against the wicked is the divine word by which Yahweh acts to bring about his purposes on the earth. That is exactly the significance of v. 14 in which someone, the prophet or, more probably perhaps, because of its intrusive position at that point and its rather different emphasis on the 'glory' of God, a later commentator, has seen that the ultimate aim of God's purpose is no less than a different world, filled with the knowledge of God's 'glory', in which his universal presence is recognized.

As we have seen, many commentators have questioned the originality of the psalm of ch. 3. This is partly because of its separate superscription, 'a prayer (*'t^ephillâh*) of Habakkuk', a type of heading which, with different ascriptions, is found frequently in the Psalter (e.g. Pss. 17, 86, 90, 102, 142), and the musical direction at the end, again similar to those found throughout the Psalter (e.g. Pss. 4, 6, 54, 55). It is significant that there is no mention of ch. 3 in the commentary on Habakkuk found at Qumran.

Finally, some have failed to see any logical connection between chs. 1–2 and this final chapter. However, Haak has shown that we cannot deduce from the fact of its omission from 1QpHab that this final chapter was unknown at Qumran. A manuscript of the twelve minor prophets was discovered as early as 1955 at Wadi Murabba'at, about 17 km south of Qumram, which does contain the chapter. Further, the new superscription and the apparent lack of logical development of thought look very different once we view the material in the book as a whole as of cultic origin. Just as the woes of ch. 2 may be seen as effecting the promise of Yahweh made to the prophet in the vision oracle of 2.1-5, so the psalm of ch. 3 may be another way of announcing the final victory of Yahweh over all his enemies in a way familiar from the cult. As such it would have to be seen as yet further prophetic confirmation of the certainty of the promise of the vision oracle.

W.F. Albright made a detailed study of the psalm in which he saw a complex, but coherent, structure. Verse 2 forms the first part. Albright saw this as an ancient prayer for the prolongation of the king's life, a prayer of the same order as a hymn to Ishtar for the life of Ammiditana (dated about 1600 BCE). However, in directing it towards Yahweh the author has used it for his own purpose. This view has not been followed by all and, in fact, the Hebrew of v. 2 is obscure.

M.L. Barré followed Hiebert in seeing ch. 3 as a victory hymn
and rendered v. 2 as follows:

> Yahweh, I have heard of your reputation,
> I have been awestruck, Yahweh, by your work.
> In the battle of yore you declared it,
> In the battle of yore you made it known,
> In your ancient fury you proclaimed it.

The literal meaning is not important. It is natural that, as in
many psalms of the Psalter, Yahweh's former glorious deeds
are recalled with the prayer, implicit or explicit, that they be
renewed (e.g. Pss. 75.1 [2]; 85.1-4 [2-5], and, on a personal
level, 22.3-5 [4-6]). Since the whole purpose of recalling these
deeds of Yahweh in the liturgy of the temple is to renew the
experience of them in the present and to draw hope from
them for the future (see Mowinckel on the function of the
'Enthronement Psalms' in this respect) we may take it that
this is the function of v. 2, whatever precise allusions are, or
are not, to be found in it. The second part for Albright consists
of vv. 3-7 and is an early Israelite poem about the theophany
('appearance' or 'coming to his people') of Yahweh, for which
we have early parallels in such passages as Judg. 5.4; Deut.
33.2ff.; Ps. 68.7-8 (8-9). The psalm of Habakkuk and these
other passages share a common tradition that Yahweh comes
from the southern regions. Verses 8-15 form the third part of
the psalm; and Albright found so many parallels to Canaanite
religious epics and mythological themes here that he believed
it to have been adapted from a Canaanite poem. Originally
this celebrated the triumph of Ba'al over Judge River, Prince
Yam ('sea') and Mot ('death'). These were all variant names of
the single, primordial chaos monster which, in the Babylonian
literature, was known as Tiamat. Day has also found many
Canaanite parallels in these verses. Both Albright and Day
rejected Irwin's earlier assertion that the mythological allusions
in this chapter were influenced by Babylonian sources rather
than Canaanite. The balance of opinion favours Albright and
Day, but since such ideas had already been crystallized in the
cult of the temple of Jerusalem (cf. Pss. 74.13-17; 77.16-20
[17-21], 89.9-14 [10-15]) the direct sources of inspiration need
not concern us here. The fourth and final part (vv. 16-19),

which according to Albright was poetically inferior and innocent of Canaanite influences, was from a different hand. This might have gone back to the original prophet Habakkuk.

We need not follow Albright in his efforts to date the psalm by its poetic style and alleged historical allusions to the period between 605 and 589 BCE. Rather, its clear cultic habitat shows that, like the material in the remainder of the book, it uses deliberately general and metaphorical language so that it could be applied in, and found relevant to, many different situations of need. However, there is no doubt that vv. 16-19, with their reversion to the first-person speech of the prophet, do bind the psalm in with the rest of the book. The prophet, who has complained at the injustice of his situation, and who has been told to wait for the vision, here announces his determination to wait through the present time of distress, confident however that the promise of the vision oracle will be fulfilled. These verses are very much in the spirit of Isa. 8.16-17, in which the prophet announces his intention to wait for Yahweh through a time when he appears to be hiding his face from his people. His wait, however, is in hope, for in the oracle of 2.4-5, in the utterance of the woes against all forms of injustice in 2.6-20 and in the cultic celebration of Yahweh's primordial victory over the powers of chaos in the psalm of ch. 3, he is confident that all is soon to be renewed and the promises fulfilled.

The function of the book of Habakkuk is thus seen to be a cultic one; and, as such, the exact identity of its author, if such a term be appropriate, is not of moment. That is not to say that it is a 'prophetic liturgy' complete as it stands (contra Haak). It is not to deny that it may have reached its present form by a series of additions and, indeed, by a quite complex process of development. It is to say, however, that the prayer and words which were provoked by the difficult situation of the late seventh century BCE were uttered in such a way and in such language that they could be found to be appropriate and effective in many other such situations. It is the material of worship in which lament, prophetic oracle, the utterance of woes and the reminder of the great liturgical acts in the temple all had their place. In these, Yahweh's victory over the primordial forces of chaos was recalled, renewed and found to be the basis of future hope. As such the material could continue to act as a powerful means of expression of the religious faith of the people. That it did so is clear to us, not just from our deductions from its general language and cultic forms, but from the actual encouragement that the covenanters of Qumran drew from it and from the power of its message for St Paul.

The prophetic spirit breathes through this work: the spirit of indignation against all forms of human oppression and injustice, against all power structures which deny the weak and poor their rights. But there breathes through it also the prophetic confidence in the justice and power of God which can inform a lively hope, even in the blackest times when justice seems most darkly obscured by present wrong, that God's intention for his people is a new order in which evil is overcome. It is the expression also of the prophetic confidence in God's power ultimately to effect that purpose through all the earth.

Further Reading

W.F. Albright, 'The Psalm of Habakkuk', in H.H. Rowley (ed.), *Studies in Old Testament Prophecy* (Edinburgh: T. & T. Clark, 1950).

M.L. Barré, 'Habakkuk 3:2: Translation in Context', *CBQ* 50 (1988), pp. 184-97.

W.H. Brownlee, 'The Placarded Revelation of Habakkuk', *JBL* 82 (1963), pp. 319-25.

J. Day, 'Echoes of Baal's Seven Thunders and Lightnings in Psalm XXIX and Habakkuk III 9 and the Identity of the Seraphim in Isaiah VI', *VT* 29 (1979), pp. 143-51.

—'New Light on the Mythological Background of the Allusion to Resheph in Habakkuk III 5', *VT* 29 (1979), pp. 353-55.

—*God's Conflict with the Dragon and the Sea*.

Eaton, *Vision in Worship*.

J.A. Emerton, 'The Textual and Linguistic Problem of Habakkuk II 4-5', *JTS* NS 28 (1977), pp. 1-18.

A.H.J. Gunneweg, 'Habakuk und das Problem des leidenden ṣdyq', *ZAW* 98 (1986), pp. 400-15.

J.M. Holt, 'So He May Run Who Reads It', *JBL* 83 (1964), pp. 298-303.

W.A. Irwin, 'The Psalm of Habakkuk', *JNES* 1 (1942), pp. 10-40.

—'The Mythological Background of Habakkuk Chapter 3', *JNES* 15 (1956), pp. 47-50.

J.G. Janzen, 'Habakkuk 2:2-4 in the Light of Recent Philological Advances', *HTR* 73 (1980), pp. 53-78.

A.R. Johnson, 'The Psalms', in H.H. Rowley (ed.), *The Old Testament and Modern Study* (Oxford: Clarendon Press, 1951), pp. 162-209.

R.A. Mason, *Haggai, Zechariah and Malachi* (CBC; Cambridge: Cambridge University Press, 1977).

J.M. Scott, 'A New Approach to Habakkuk ii 4-5a', *VT* 35 (1985), pp. 330-40.

P.M. Southwell, 'A Note on Hab. 2:4', *JTS* NS 19 (1968), pp. 614-17.

C. Westermann, *Basic Forms of Prophetic Speech* (trans. H.C. White; London: Lutterworth, 1967).

A.S. van der Woude, 'Der Gerechte wird durch seine Treue leben', in W.C. van Unnik and A.S. van der Woude (eds.), *Studia Biblica et Semitica T.C. Vriezen dedicata* (Wageningen: H. Veenman & Zonen, 1966).

—'Habakuk 2.4', *ZAW* 82 (1970), pp. 281-82.

Part III

JOEL

12

THE CONTENTS
OF THE BOOK OF JOEL

THE SMALL BOOK OF JOEL, consisting of only three chapters (four in the Hebrew Bible), must count as one of the most enigmatic in the 'Book of the Twelve'; although, as we have seen, the minor prophets present us with many an enigma. If justification is needed for dubbing Joel the most problematic it is to be found in the bewildering variety of scholarly interpretations of the book, which seem to differ more and more and to become more and more speculative as time goes on, and further and further away from consensus. But it would be a pity if the book's difficulties so dominated our horizon that we had no eyes for much in it that is splendid. It contains, for example, a striking call for true penitence before God.

> 'Yet even now,' says the LORD,
> 'return to me with all your heart,
> with fasting, with weeping, and with mourning;
> and rend your hearts and not your garments' (Joel 2.12-13).

Joel is often justly described as one of the 'cultic prophets'; but this, if a reminder is needed, jolts us into recognizing that such prophets could match for depth of religious insight and beauty of language any of the prophets of the Old Testament. We may cite as an example Joel 2.28-29 (Heb. 3.1-2), words familiar to Christian readers from their use as a text in the sermon of Peter at Pentecost recorded in Acts 2.17-18:

> And it shall come to pass afterward,
> that I will pour out my spirit on all flesh;
> your sons and your daughters shall prophesy,
> your old men shall dream dreams,

and your young men shall see visions.
Even upon the menservants and maidservants
in those days I will pour out my spirit.

Such a picture of the universalizing of God's gifts, recalling as
it does the words attributed to Moses in Num. 11.29, 'Would
that all the Lord's people were prophets!', shows remarkable
vision and sensitivity. It would be the height of pedantry to
become so absorbed in the problem of the date when these
words were uttered and of their relation to the earlier part of
the book that, like Bunyan's man with the muckrake, we miss
their splendour and, perhaps, even their disturbing challenge
to the establishment of the day—and of later times.

The book of Joel falls into several fairly easily identifiable
major sections:

1. 1.1: Superscription, attributing the words which follow
   to Joel son of Pethuel.
2. 1.2-4: Announcement of a swarm of locusts.
3. 1.5-14: Summons to the community and the priests to
   mourn and fast in the face of the devastation of
   nature which they are experiencing.
4. 1.15-20: Lamentation and prayer, in which the disaster is linked to 'the Day of the LORD' (v. 15).
5. 2.1-11: Call for the trumpet alarm in Zion, since an
   army (a symbol for the locusts?) is advancing on the
   capital. This also is linked to the concept of 'the Day of
   the LORD' (v. 11).
6. 2.12-14: Call for repentance by Yahweh and by the
   prophet.
7. 2.15-17: Renewed call to a cultic penitential fast with
   a prayer for use by the priests.
8. 2.18-27: Yahweh's response announcing renewed
   fertility, the defeat of 'the northerner', the gift of rain
   and his continuing presence among his people.
9. 2.28-32 (3.1-5): Signs which will accompany the 'Day
   of the LORD' (v. 31 [4]); the spirit of prophecy poured
   out on all sections of the community; cosmic upheavals,
   and salvation for those 'who call on the name of the
   LORD', who appear to be equated with 'those whom
   the LORD calls'.

10.   3(4).1-3: God will gather the nations who have oppressed his people to the valley of Jehoshaphat, and will judge them there.
11.   3(4).4-8: God will requite certain specified nations who have acted against him in acting against his people.
12.   3(4).9-17: A 'Divine Warrior' hymn summoning the nations to prepare for battle as God marches out against them and judges them from Zion, where he protects his own people.
13.   3(4).18: A picture of miraculously renewed fertility; a spring issues from the temple.
14.   3(4).19-21: A 'reversal of judgment' in which traditional enemies of Judah are desolated while Judah and Jerusalem are repopulated in security.

Behind this apparently simple structure lie a number of difficult questions which have perplexed interpreters of the book throughout the history of its investigation. It is to these that we now turn.

13

THE DISASTER THAT
THREATENS THE COMMUNITY

WHAT IS THE NATURE of this disaster? At first glance it seems
straightforward enough. 1.2-4 tells of a plague of locusts on
an unprecedented scale. Its fearfulness is suggested by the
use of four different names for locusts in 1.4; the English
versions tend to take these to denote different types of locust,
but recently some scholars have suggested that they refer to
different stages in the development of the insect from the
grub stage. However this may be, J.A. Thompson rightly
pointed out that this is one of many places in the book where
repetition seems to be used for the sake of emphasis. On the
other hand, locusts are mentioned again in the book only in
2.25; and much of the other material suggests that the real
problem was one of drought (1.17-18; 2.23), fire (1.19-20; 2.3)
or invasion by a hostile army (1.6; 2.1-11, 20). Is the reference
to locusts to be understood literally (Thompson), are they symbolic of an invading army (Stuart) or do they have some
mythological significance? (Childs is one of those who believes
they certainly came to have such significance in the course of
the book's development.) Hubbard finds the reference to
locusts to be literal in ch. 1 but figurative in ch. 2. Some
scholars (for instance Ogden) have seen all such references,
whether to locusts, fire or drought, as stock metaphors of
lament, having no particular historical reference.

The great majority of commentators, however, have had little
difficulty in seeing much of the description of the ravages of
the land in ch. 1 as the result of the locusts' stripping all
vegetation. The description in ch. 2 is different in that the

metaphor (if it be metaphor) of the invading army is pursued with great vigour and in great detail. However, we must not miss the fact that all this is vivid and forceful poetry (see below), and metaphor has a vital function in poetry. It is probable, therefore, that the locust theme is continued in this chapter. Thompson gives a number of examples of enemy armies' being likened to swarms of locusts for number and destructiveness, but maintains that locusts are never used as a symbol for human armies. He therefore believes that Joel 2 *likens* locusts to an army rather than using the locusts as a *symbol* of an army. However, metaphor can have a life of its own, and obviously could work the other way in the course of time and of the transmission of the text. Many scholars believe that the locusts do serve in the book as a whole as a symbol for the human enemies whose fate is described in chs. 3–4. The somewhat mixed poetic metaphors of chs. 1–2—of locusts, drought, fire and armies—could have been understood in a number of ways in the course of the book's development and reapplied to new and later situations. Further, if this material was intended to serve as a community lament, as Ogden and others have suggested, the language may be deliberately general, as it is in the psalms of lament, so that it could be used in a variety of circumstances. The possible cultic associations of the book of Joel are explored below.

Further Reading

B.S. Childs, 'The Enemy from the North and the Chaos Tradition', *JBL* 68 (1959), pp. 187-98.

D.A. Hubbard, *Joel and Amos: An Introduction and Commentary* (TOTC; London: Tyndale Press, 1989).

G.S. Ogden, 'Joel 4 and Prophetic Responses to National Laments', *JSOT* 26 (1983), pp. 97-106.

G.S. Ogden (with R.R. Deutsch), *Joel and Malachi*.

Stuart, *Hosea–Jonah*.

J.A. Thompson, 'Joel's Locusts in the Light of Near Eastern Parallels', *JNES* 14 (1955), pp. 52-55.

—'The Use of Repetition in the Prophecy of Joel', in M. Black and W. Smalley (eds.), *Language, Culture and Religion: In Honour of Eugene A. Nida* (The Hague, 1974), pp. 101-110.

14

THE UNITY OF
THE BOOK OF JOEL

SINCE THE LATER PART of the nineteenth century many scholars have questioned the unity of the book of Joel. Allen and Prinsloo both give useful summaries of the history of criticism. That the mood of the book changes at 2.18 is generally agreed. Up to that point, as the summary above indicates, two passages have depicted and lamented the sufferings of the land and its people and called on priests and people to join in penitential fasts which would represent a genuine return to God. A change of fortune is hinted at as a possibility (but not a certainty) in 2.14. The ravages caused by the locusts are seen as the first signs of a coming 'Day of the LORD' (1.15; 2.11) which is depicted in traditional prophetic terms as a day of darkness and destruction for Yahweh's own people (1.15-18; 2.10-11). Amos had made such a concept of the Day of Yahweh part of the pre-exilic prophetic tradition (Amos 5.18-20; cf. Isa. 2.12); one of his visions, interestingly, is of judgment by means of a swarm of locusts which is, however, averted by the prophet's intercession (Amos 7.1-3).

In contrast with many other prophetic books, Joel does not specify any of the sins which have brought about this divine judgment; confession of specific sins does not seem to belong to the 'lament' genre in the Old Testament (see above). That the catastrophe is due to the people's sin is however made clear in Joel by the call to penitential fasts and the summons to 'return to me with all your heart' which the prophet issues in the name of Yahweh (2.12-13).

The exact relation between the sufferings and 'the Day of

the LORD' in these opening two chapters has been the subject of some discussion among scholars. For Ahlström the sufferings are the signs of the Day which is to follow—a view earlier held by T.H. Robinson; for D.R. Jones the plague of locusts is described as a past event, but as one which points to a Day of Yahweh yet to come; while for L.C. Allen it is a contemporary manifestation of the Day. Some who have argued for a discontinuity between the two parts of the book have suggested that the two references to the Day of the LORD in chs. 1–2 are a later insertion intended to link the locust plague with the more 'apocalyptic' section 2.28–3.21 (chs. 3–4). Amos, however, saw the many judgments which had apparently been falling on the land and people of Israel over a considerable period of time (cf. 4.6-11) as foreshadowing the coming Day of Yahweh; and there seems little difficulty in supposing that Joel also could have conceived of contemporary events as bearing a similar significance.

With 2.18, however, the tone of the book changes completely. In 2.18-27 Yahweh announces in first-person speech his promise to save his people—apparently without exception—so that 'my people shall never again be put to shame' (2.27). Thereafter the depiction of the Day of Yahweh is quite different from that of 1.2–2.17. In 2.28-32 (3.1-5) Yahweh will renew his people by his spirit, while cosmic upheavals (often the accompaniment of God's final victory over the forces of chaos in the more eschatological Old Testament literature) usher in God's deliverance on Mount Zion of those who 'call on his name', described as 'those who are delivered' and who 'escape'—that is, apparently, *not* everyone. In ch. 3 (Heb. 4) the Day of Yahweh is, as in chs. 1–2, a day of divine judgment; but now God judges not his own people but the oppressor nations, whom he brings to the valley of Jehoshaphat for this purpose (3[4].1-3, 14-16). His own people are now under his protection (3.16-17); and, while other nations become the desolate wilderness that the locusts, drought and invasion had once made Judah (3.19-21), Judah itself is to become a land of paradisiacal plenty (3.18). 'The Day' is still a day of darkness; but whereas in 2.10 this was because the swarming numbers of the locusts blotted out the light, now it is because of the cosmic upheavals which will accompany God's final acts of salvation (3[4].15). Whereas God's favour was only a possibility in 1.14, it is now a firmly assured divine promise (2.19-27, 37; 3[4].16-17). Whereas in 1.2–2.17 present events are seen as harbingers of the Day which is coming, in 2.28–3.21 (Heb. 3.1–4.21) the phenomena which accompany the Day have no apparent immediate historical precursor but are acts of God which he will perform at some unspecified time in the future.

It is issues such as these that have led many commentators to question the unity of the book. The first to have done so appears to have been M. Vernes; he was followed by J.W. Rothstein, who in 1896 translated and annotated a German edition of S.R. Driver's *Introduction to the Literature of the Old Testament*, first published in 1891. Rothstein believed that the first part of the book of Joel is pre-exilic, but that 2.28–3.21 (Heb. 3.1–4.21) was added only after the exile. B. Duhm saw Joel's hand only as far as 2.17, while a later apocalyptic writer added the remainder, together with the 'Day of Yahweh' references in the first part. E. Sellin, J.A. Bewer, T.H. Robinson and O. Eissfeldt substantially shared this position. Among later writers to voice a similar view have been B.S. Childs, who believed that a later editor made Joel's words into an apocalyptic-type picture of the end, O. Kaiser and A. Soggin. O. Loretz has recently argued that the book as we have it must be the result of a lengthy process of additions and expansions. A somewhat similar point of view is that of S. Bergler, who does see the book as the work of one writer, but one who used existing traditional material including a poem describing a drought and another describing an enemy invasion. Quoting from these and other, older biblical traditions such as the Exodus plague tradition and the 'foe from the north' tradition, he sees Joel as bringing a message to his post-exilic contemporaries showing them that the present distress which they are undergoing calls for repentance, for it has eschatological significance. Whether or not one accepts his idea of a scribal exegete at work in the book, Bergler's suggestion that older material may have been reworked and reapplied in new situations is an important one.

A most interesting challenge to the unity of the book was made by O. Plöger. The main thesis of his book was that, after the exile, two main streams of religious thought developed in Judah. The first was that expressed by the Priestly writing of the Pentateuch and by the Chronicler. Those writers believed that with the re-establishment of the temple, presided over by the duly and divinely appointed priestly, levitical and singing orders, with Torah at the centre of the community's life as a defining, guiding and controlling force, the ancient purposes of God for his people had already been realized within this world's history. The fulfilment of the promises of the prophets consisted for these Priestly writers in the existence of a theocracy rather than in the nation as a political entity. Such a view might be described in more recent times as 'a realized eschatology'—that is, a belief that God's purposes for his people have been fulfilled here and now. Against that, however, were those who became increasingly dissatisfied with the contemporary state of affairs, and who believed that the prophetic promises presaged something much more drastic. They believed that it was God's purpose to intervene in this world's history in a new and decisive way, overturning this world's powers and establishments, so bringing in a new age and a new kingdom of a kind not yet experienced. Plöger traces what he sees as the evidence for this 'eschatological' party in the book of Daniel, Isaiah 24–27, Zechariah 12–14 and the book of Joel. In his treatment of the last of these he states his belief that chs. 1–2 have the character of much pre-exilic prophecy. They refer to locusts and drought as contemporary historical events and, like Amos, link these to the Day of Yahweh. However, as is the way of prophecy, this Day of Yahweh is not presented as an immutable, long predicted final act at the end of time, but as an action of God within present history. As such it is contingent, not determined, and could be averted by penitence and cultic measures undertaken to secure Yahweh's help. However, after the exile the 'eschatological' party added ch. 3 (Heb. 4), portraying the 'Day of Yahweh' as a universal and decisive action of God when he would overthrow the present kingdoms of this world and establish his own new kingdom. 2.28-32 (Heb. 3.1-5) was then added later still to show that this was not for all Israel. It was only for those who 'call on the name of Yahweh', only those whom God had called, who would form the remnant. This group was, of course, the eschatological party, those who had the insight to discern the eschatological significance of God's actions and who thus were not deceived into thinking that the present theocratic establishment was the ultimate fulfilment of God's purpose.

This hypothesis has the merit of taking seriously the apparent qualification in 2.32 (3.5) of those who may expect salvation. It accounts also for the sharpening eschatological expectation of the final two chapters of the book. However, like much of Plöger's exegesis, its results depend a great deal on a prior assumption about the existence of two such parties in post-exilic Judah. That there were differences of emphasis seems certain, but that the break between the two was as total as the theory demands is not clear from the biblical literature. The theocrats may well have had hopes of something beyond the present order, while the eschatological party certainly seems to have evinced strong cultic and temple links. Why else should the apocalyptists of 2.28–3.21 (Heb. 3.1–4.21) have retained the first part of this book with its strong call for the cultic expression of true repentance? And which book more than Daniel, the most 'apocalyptic' of all the Old Testament writings, has evinced such 'theocratic' interests as strict observance of the dietary laws, prayer three times a day, and the eventual renewal of the twice daily sacrifices in the temple? Nevertheless, Plöger has thrown into clear relief the differences between the two parts of the book of Joel which have led so many other scholars to question its unity.

But the unity of the book has not been without its strong supporters. Indeed, if such matters were to be settled by numbers of protagonists to be found on each side, its unity could probably be guaranteed. One scholar who argues for the unity of the book is W. Rudolph, who maintains that the description of the locust plague in ch. 1 is so terrifying that the prophet must have seen it as the precursor of the Day of Yahweh. He calls priests and people to lamentation and prayer, for God alone can avert the distress. In 2.1-17 he stresses the threatening eschatological aspect of this plague of locusts. That is why the penitential fast is so important: it is the only way to salvation. The result of the fast is shown in 2.18. Here Yahweh responds to the people's penitence by showing grace (1.14 demonstrates that this was no more than a possibility before their 'return to him'). 2.19-20 is an oracle assuring the people that their prayers have been heard; 2.21-24 is a summons to thanksgiving for this, while 2.25-27 contains a further oracle of promise. This divine response is taken further in 2.28–3.21 (Heb. 3.1–4.21). The Day of Yahweh remains a terrible reality; but now it affects only the heathen. This is all a fulfilment of the promise of 2.26b-27, as is shown by 2.32 (3.5) ('as the LORD has said...'). These passages are all the work of the one prophet. Only 3(4).4-8 is later, and even that may be the work of the same hand, perhaps intended for another place; or, as others have argued, it may be a later, specific application of the promises to an existing historical situation.

Another scholar who has argued strongly for the substantial unity of the book is H.W. Wolff. He sees Joel as one who deliberately took prophetic themes from the past such as 'the Day of Yahweh' and 'the foe from the north', in order to show that God's promises for his people are still valid and effective. Chapter 1 tells of a locust plague which took place in the past but which is presented as an omen of future disaster and which invites the people to renewed communal lament in order to avert this. The invasion of ch. 2 relates to a different situation: the assault of an alien army now imminent and threatening a final judgment for Judah and Jerusalem. This can be avoided only by repentance. Hence the urgency of 2.12: 'Yet *even now* if you return...' The people cannot rely on a repetition of past escapes. So the 'Day of Yahweh' references of chs. 1–2, far from being later insertions, show the real relation between the two events. That which was threatened in earlier prophecy is now at hand. If, however, Israel now repents, the Day will change from one of judgment against Israel to one of salvation for its people and judgment on those who are threatening them; and that is the theme of the second part of the book.

Wolff further supports his arguments for unity by a list of 'catchword' parallels between the two parts. Examples of these are: the 'sanctify' and 'call' of 1.14 and 3(4).9; 'the day is near' of 1.15, 2.1 and 3(4).14; the 'darkness' of the day in 2.2 and 2.31 (3.4); the 'gather the people' of 2.16 and 3(4).2, 11. In addition to these and several other such links he adduces thematic parallels. These can be found in the lament over the scarcity of food in 1.4-20 and the promise of reversal in 2.21-27; the imminence of disaster for Jerusalem of 2.1-11 and the restoration of the city of 3(4).1-3, 9-17; the call to return to Yahweh as the necessity of the moment of 2.12-17 and the promise of the outpouring of the spirit as an eschatological necessity in 2.28-29 (3.1-2).

A number of other scholars who defend the unity of the book have been much impressed by such a list of corresponding words and ideas between the two parts; for example Hubbard and, to some extent, Keller (who speaks of 'the evocative power of the images, the style, the thought' which 'all remain the same'), Ogden and Stuart. However, it is too often over-looked that such correspondences can be redactional, as Childs observed. An example of this is the extraordinary number of 'mirror image' reversals of fortune for Jerusalem between Micah 3 and 4–5 (see Mason). Few, however, would argue for identity of authorship of these chapters of Micah.

Others who have argued for the essential unity of the book have done so on the grounds of its cultic nature and use. A.S. Kapelrud saw the book as having been built up as a liturgy exactly like many of the psalms of lament, in which lamentation is followed by Yahweh's answer in the form of a prophetic oracle (for the form of such psalms see above). He understood the laments of chs. 1–2, with their call to peni-tence, as two such liturgies. 2.18-27 is the oracular answer in Yahweh's name, assuring the congregation that their prayers have been heard. Their penitence has averted the threatened judgment, and now Yahweh's salvation is promised. 2.28-32 (3.1-5) and 3(4).1-21 are continuations of Yahweh's answer. The many parallels with other prophetic sayings (see below) may suggest 'a common cultic source'—an idea also suggested by Coggins.

A not dissimilar view was expressed by G.W. Ahlström. While he is cautious about whether or not the book as it stands is a liturgy, he maintains that 'it is beyond doubt that Joel has made use of liturgical forms, phrases and formulas'. The book is aimed at establishing 'right order' ($ṣ^edāqâ$) for Yahweh's people. This can only be brought about by a right covenant relationship with Yahweh in which all the covenant commands are kept. But this has consequences for the created world with its ordered seasons maintained by Yahweh's victory over the forces of chaos, as in the ancient Near Eastern myths. So the cult's function is to establish, maintain and, where necessary, restore this right order among people and in the created world. So Ahlström says:

> In the book of Joel the present historical situation or reality has been so combined with the cultic that they are inseparable. The right cult is the only foundation for the future of the people.

This 'right cult' expresses the people's true penitence, but also has as its consequences Yahweh's victory over the forces of chaos—hence the 'war' imagery of the book of Joel and the picture of final salvation as the defeat by Yahweh of all his, and his people's, enemies. This means, therefore, that laments, calls for penitence and eschatological promises all belong together in a cultic unity. (For a recent study of such themes see Murray).

More recently G.S. Ogden has argued for a unity of the book viewed as a series of prophetic answers to national laments. He too sees striking parallels with the psalms of lament, including the general and mixed nature of the metaphors of drought, fire, invasion and the like, which do not function as 'a factual account of the problem faced', but serve more general cultic purposes. The book itself is not a liturgy but what he describes as a 'literary work arising from such a liturgical background'. Its probable setting was an attack by foreign nations. C.A. Keller also saw the work as inspired by 'liturgical reminiscences' while not being itself a liturgy. Other similar views are expressed by K.S. Nash, who believed that the book served as a call to a penitential assembly in the face of severe climactic conditions, J.D. Watts, who believed it to have had a festival setting, and W. Rudolph, who agrees that Joel was a cult prophet.

To this we shall have to return when we consider possible cultic associations of the book. There can be no doubt that recognition of the influence of the cult on the book is important if we are to understand its nature and function. However, to allow that the divine oracles of 2.28–3.21 (Heb. 3.1–4.21) serve in the present book as oracular answers to the laments and prayers of chs. 1–2 does not necessarily imply that the whole book was the product of one person at one time. This is clear from the work of O. Loretz, who sees its roots in cultic rituals designed to secure the gift of rain from Yahweh. However, for him, the present book is the result of a series of editorial expansions which build on this. So, for example, the description of the invasion by an alien army in 2.1-11a and the Day of Yahweh passages were added in order to invest the situation of drought with eschatological significance. The final part of the book saw further expansions in which the gift of rain by Yahweh in answer to the prayers of his people becomes symbolic of his purposes for their future salvation.

Further Reading

G.W. Ahlström, *Joel and the Temple Cult of Jerusalem* (VTSup, 21; Leiden: Brill, 1971).

Allen, *The Books of Joel, Obadiah, Jonah and Micah*.

S. Bergler, *Joel als Schriftinterpret* (Beiträge zur Erforschung des Alten Testaments und das Antiken Judentums, 16; Frankfurt: Peter Lang, 1988).

R.J. Coggins, 'An Alternative Prophetic Tradition?', in R.J. Coggins *et al.* (eds.), *Israel's Prophetic Tradition* (Cambridge: Cambridge University Press, 1982).

S.R. Driver, *Einleitung in die Literatur des alten Testaments* (ed. and trans. J.W. Rothstein: Berlin: Reuther, 1896).

B. Duhm, 'Anmerkungen zu den zwölf Propheten', *ZAW* 31 (1911), pp. 184-88.

O. Eissfeldt, *The Old Testament: An Introduction* (trans. P.R. Ackroyd; Oxford: Basil Blackwell, 1965).

Jones, *Isaiah 55–66 and Joel*.

O. Kaiser, *Introduction to the Old Testament* (trans. J. Sturdy; Oxford: Basil Blackwell, 1975).

A.S. Kapelrud, *Joel Studies* (Uppsala: Lundequistska Bokhandeln, 1948).

Keller, *Osée, Joel, Abdias, Jonas, Amos.*

O. Loretz, *Regenritual und Jahwetag im Joelbuch* (Ugaritic-Biblische Literatur, 4; Altenberger, Soest, 1986).

R. Murray, *The Cosmic Covenant* (London: Sheed & Ward, 1992).

K.S. Nash, 'The Cycle of Seasons in Joel', *The Bible Today* 27 (1989), p. 74-80.

O. Plöger, *Theocracy and Eschatology* (trans. S. Rudman; Oxford: Basil Blackwell, 1968).

W.S. Prinsloo, *The Theology of the Book of Joel* (Berlin: de Gruyter, 1985).

T.H. Robinson (with F. Horst), *Die Zwölf Kleinen Propheten* (HAT, 1.14; Tübingen: Mohr, 3rd edn, 1964).

Rudolph, *Joel, Amos, Obadja, Jona.*

E. Sellin, *Das Zwölfprophetenbuch* (KAT, 12.1; Gütersloh, 3rd edn, 1930).

Smith (with Ward and Bewer), *Zephaniah, Micah, Zechariah, Nahum, Habakkuk, Obadiah, Joel.*

J.A. Soggin, *Introduction to the Old Testament* (London; SCM Press, 1976).

M. Vernes, *Le peuple d'Israël et ses espérances relatives à son avenir depuis les origines jusqu'à l'époque persane (Ve siècle avant JC)* (Paris: Sandoz & Fischbacher, 1872).

H.W. Wolff, *Joel and Amos* (Hermeneia; Philadelphia: Fortress Press, 1977).

15

THE DATING OF
THE BOOK OF JOEL

THE DATE OF THE BOOK has proved an even thornier problem than that of its unity, dates having been offered all the way from the ninth century BCE (M. Bič) right down to the late fourth century (M. Treves). While there is a fairly general consensus for the post-exilic period, and perhaps for an early date in that period, the bewildering variety of views suggests either that scholars have been asking the wrong questions of the text or that in some cases their logic is faulty. Butterworth concluded simply that the evidence for dating the book is inconclusive. The book's position in the canon is not informative on this point, since it was probably placed where it is because of its strong links with the book of Amos (cf. Dennefeld and Wolff).

The book itself offers no explicit historical allusions. The superscription tells us only the name of Joel's father, and gives no hint of the kings in whose reign he was active. 3(4).4-8 does refer to the actions of some specific cities and peoples (Tyre, Sidon, Philistia, the Greeks, the Sabeans), while Egypt and Edom are mentioned in 3(4).19; but even if these allusions are clear enough for the purpose of dating (and that is questionable), there is little agreement as to whether these verses are original to the book or added later. Indeed, even to discuss 'the date of the book' begs the question in favour of its unity, which is itself, as we have seen, highly disputable. Examples of 'asking the wrong questions' of the text and thus of getting dubious answers abound in the critical literature. Such questions are asked when the literary genre of a passage is ignored and the text treated as giving factual historical information. Thus some have taken the description of the invaders in 2.9 ('They leap upon the city, they run upon the walls') as evidence for a time after Nehemiah who rebuilt the walls of Jerusalem. Not much better are those who have rejected this argument, but only because, they maintain, the walls were not completely razed to the ground even before Nehemiah's time. Both of these groups have taken lively, imaginative poetic description as a kind of video-recording of actual historical events. One scholar (F.R. Stephenson), taking such phrases as 'The sun shall be turned into darkness' (2.31 [3.4]) to refer to an eclipse of the sun, concluded that only two such eclipses (in 357 and 336 BCE) could have been meant. He completely overlooked the possibility that such language might be symbolic. Cosmic disorders and unnatural happenings traditionally mark the great final acts of God in apocalyptic literature. One could wish that some scholars would spend a little more time reading poetry!

Most of the arguments used—setting aside such heavily pedantic ones—are in fact inconclusive. A careful survey of them is found in the works of J.A. Thompson and L.C. Allen, and it would be tedious to attempt to reproduce them exhaustively here. For example, Bič drew on Ugaritic parallels for his early dating, and so did Kapelrud for his date of c. 600 BCE; but it must be asked when such ideas were assimilated into the Jerusalem cult and for how long they continued to be influential. The absence of references to a king may indicate a uniform post-exilic date for the book, but if the genre is that of the psalms of lament, we may question whether any explicit reference to a king is to be expected, since we seldom find them in those psalms. Arguments based on references to the priests are also faulty. The priests who are so prominent in the book no doubt exercised a more prominent role in the temple after the exile than they did before, but the Jerusalem priesthood was certainly not a post-exilic invention. The Zadokites were influential there from the time of Solomon onwards. In fact, it is difficult to find anything in chs. 1–2 which demands a post-exilic date.

The many parallels in the book to other biblical material are highly significant, and I shall consider them in the following section. But not all of these imply a late date. Some scholars have suggested that Joel may be the original of some of the passages shared with other books. It is highly unlikely that this book, more than any other in the Old Testament, should have become a source of citation for a wide variety of biblical writers, as has been implied. It is far more probable that Joel was drawing on earlier material. But even here one must exercise caution. We do not always know whether a similarity is due to a deliberate quotation from another author, or whether two or more may be drawing on traditional prophetic material. This has almost certainly happened with the oracle common to Isaiah and Micah (Isa. 2.2-4 = Mic. 4.1-4). See my discussion of this elsewhere and the remarks of R.J. Coggins alluded to above.

Alleged verbal parallels with other books are also a suspect method by which to date Joel. Resemblances have been claimed with Elijah and Moses (Bič), Jeremiah (Kapelrud), Ezekiel (Mariès) and Second Isaiah and Malachi (Chary). If in fact Joel draws on language and imagery familiar from the cult, this could account for parallels with other books similarly influenced. Parallel ideas and circumstances have also been found with Malachi and Zechariah 9–14. These will be examined later; but they certainly make a post-exilic date more probable for the final form of the book.

There remain historical allusions. The people of Tyre, Sidon and Philistia are accused in 3(4).4-8 of plundering God's people and selling them abroad into slavery to the Greeks. God, in requiting them, will cause them to be captured by Judaeans and sold in turn to the Sabeans. This may refer to some specific incident or series of incidents, but we have to remember that the Phoenicians and Philistians had a long history of antagonism towards Israel, and that Greek traders had no doubt been active all round the eastern Mediterranean coast long before the conquests of Alexander the Great. Again, the Sabeans had been known to Israel over a long period and arc particularly noted in the Old Testament for their trading activities. Ezek. 27.22 mentions them as such, interestingly in connection with Tyre. Ps. 72.10, 15 even envisages the Sabeans bringing tribute to the Davidic king.

All this is quite enough to suggest that traditional and familiar themes are employed in these passages in Joel in a general way to indicate the reversal of fortunes when God acts to deliver his people, bringing down their traditional oppressors and requiting them with just the kind of fate to which they had subjected his people. However, the sharp differences between these verses and their context, with the former actually specifying particular peoples while elsewhere in the book they are referred to only generally as 'the nations', may point to a later attempt to apply the promises of the book to a particular historical context. But insufficient details are given for us to be able to identify these references with any confidence. Certainly the reference to Egypt and to Edom in 3(4).19 again seems to be of a quite general kind in which traditional enemies are seen as typifying the fate which awaits all oppressor nations.

All this is rather negative. The date of the book of Joel remains a mystery. We can summarize the discussion, however, by saying that nothing demands a post-exilic date for 1.1–2.27. The thoughts, biblical parallels and eschatological expectations of 2.28–3.21 (Heb. 3.1–4.21) probably suggest a continuing application of the warnings and promises of the laments and answering oracle of the first part of the book to successive situations after the exile. But we are dealing with a balance of probabilities rather than with certainties.

Further Reading

M. Bič, *Das Buch Joel* (Berlin: Evangelische Verlagsanstalt, 1960).

M. Butterworth, 'The Date of the Book of Joel' (PhD dissertation, University of Nottingham, 1971).

T. Chary, *Les prophètes et le culte à partir de l'exil* (Tournai: Desclée, 1955).

L. Dennefeld, 'Les problèmes du livre de Joël', *RSR* 6 (1926), pp. 26-49.

L. Mariès, 'A propos de récentes études sur Joël', *RSR* 20 (1950), pp. 121-24.

F.R. Stephenson, 'The Date of the Book of Joel', *VT* 19 (1969), pp. 224-29.

J.A. Thompson, 'The Date of Joel', in H. Bream *et al.* (eds.), *A Light Unto My Path: OT Studies in Honour of J.M. Myers* (Philadelphia: Temple University Press, 1974), pp. 453-64.

M. Treves, 'The Date of Joel', *VT* 7 (1957), pp. 149-56.

16

PARALLELS WITH OTHER
OLD TESTAMENT MATERIAL

THERE ARE A STRIKING number of parallels with other biblical literature in the book of Joel; and, since since these must certainly influence any final assessment of the meaning and function of the book, it is necessary to devote a short chapter to them.

There are, first, some almost identical verbal parallels. Joel 1.15 reads:

> Alas for the day,
> for near is the day of Yahweh:
> as destruction from the Almighty it comes.

With this we may compare Isa. 13.6:

> Wail, for near is the day of Yahweh:
> as destruction from the Almighty it comes.

Both these verses employ a striking play on words in Hebrew, for the word 'destruction' (*šōd*) has a similar sound to the main element in the word 'Almighty' (*šaddai*). In Isaiah 13 the picture is of Yahweh coming at the head of his heavenly host to judge the earth, a judgment which will cause cosmic upheavals in which 'the sun will be dark at its rising' and 'the moon will not shed its light'. Whatever the original force and setting of this 'Divine Warrior hymn', in its present context it is related to the destruction of Babylon, which can hardly have been its original function if it occurred in the preaching of Isaiah of Jerusalem in the eighth century when Assyria was the great enemy. In Joel its use invests the plagues of locusts, drought and fire with more than passing significance.

They too are judgments of Yahweh, directed in this case, as in Amos, against his own people and his own land. It is the connection between this verse and cosmic upheavals in both Isaiah 13 and the later parts of the book of Joel (especially 2.30-31 [3.3-4]) which has led some commentators to see the 'Day of Yahweh' references in chs. 1–2 as later insertions. This may be so; but it is equally possible that the later author of Joel 2.28-32 (3.1-5) has seen the connection, and has linked Joel's plagues with the great event of Yahweh's dramatic intervention in the end days.

Another parallel is found between Joel 2.32 (3.5), 'For in Mount Zion and in Jerusalem there shall be a remnant (*pᵉlētâh*)', and Obad. v. 17: 'and in Mount Zion there shall be a remnant (*pᵉlētâh*)'. The Obadiah context also is one of 'the Day of Yahweh', which is seen as a day of Yahweh's judgment against the nations, requiting them for what they have done to his people. Although Joel 2.28-32 (3.1-5) does not explicitly mention judgment against the nations, its close parallel with the cosmic upheavals described in Isaiah 13 suggests that it belongs to this complex of ideas. While Obadiah describes those who do escape (the word carries the idea of 'survivors') as becoming 'holy', Joel explicitly describes them as 'those who call on the name of the LORD', who are also described as 'those whom the LORD calls'. This may reflect a somewhat more divided community, or may at least be an implied exhortation to those addressed to make sure they are among the 'survivors'.

In 3.10 (4.10) there is an ironic reversal of the oracle of promise common to both Isaiah and Micah. They had predicted that Yahweh's just reign would be one of universal peace, with all nations learning and obeying Torah. No international conflict would be possible, since all would submit their disputes to Yahweh's judgment which would be truly just:

> He shall judge between the nations
> and shall decide for many peoples;
> and they shall beat their swords into ploughshares,
> and their spears into pruning hooks (Isa. 2.4 = Mic. 4.3).

Joel, on the other hand, describing the onslaught of Yahweh in judgment against the nations, calls on them to prepare for battle, thus hastening their own inevitable defeat:

> Beat your ploughshares into swords,
> and your pruning hooks into spears;
> let the weak say, 'I am a warrior' (Joel 3.10).

There are also parallels between Joel and Amos. Joel 3(4).16 echoes the opening words of Amos:

> And the LORD roars from Zion
> and utters his voice from Jerusalem.

In Amos the verse introduces a series of oracles against the nations, although the ultimate intention is to denounce Israel. In Joel the verse appears to be used in a similar way, in announcing Yahweh's terrible judgment on the nations. In fact, however, its purpose is quite different: Yahweh's purpose is to protect his own people, not to denounce them.

Joel 3(4).18 contains a promise of paradisiacal fertility and plenty following Yahweh's intervention. Part of this exactly echoes Amos 9.13:

> the mountains shall drip sweet wine,
> and all the hills shall flow with it

> the mountains shall drip sweet wine
> and the hills shall flow with milk (Joel 3[4].18; a
> different verb is used in the second line).

All this suggests the existence of what might be called 'stock' prophetic oracles which could be, and often were, re-used and, like sermon material today, put to different exegetical purposes to suit the immediate situation.

Apart from such striking verbal parallels, there are a number of what might be called prophetic ideas or even prophetic images in the book of Joel which are also found elsewhere in the prophetic collections. Amos is further echoed in his depiction of 'the Day of Yahweh' as a day of darkness and judgment for God's own people. In 2.20, in the divine oracle which answers the laments and prayers of the people, another prophetic topic is re-used:

> And the northerner
> I will remove far from you,
> and I will drive him to a land,
> parched and desolate.

In the early oracles of Jeremiah (for example 1.13-16; 6.1, 22) this 'foe from the north' is a prominent feature in speaking of judgment against Israel. (The identity of those referred to or the possible mythological overtone of the allusion is discussed above.)

Finally we should not miss the clear parallels of thought, rather than of exact expression, between the book of Joel and Zechariah 9–14. There also we have the idea of God's bringing the nations against Judah and Jerusalem. In 12.1–13.6 he is said to bring them there in order to judge and destroy them; but in ch. 14 they are permitted to execute a more terrible judgment against his people and his city (vv. 2-3) before he comes as the divine warrior with all his 'holy ones' to defeat and judge the nations and rule as universal king in Zion. There he re-establishes the natural order (vv. 6-8), brings the divine gift of rain for all who worship him (v. 17) and makes Jerusalem holy again (vv. 21-22). Indeed, Zechariah 9–14 is greatly concerned with the gift of rain (10.1) and attacks the false leaders of the people who turn elsewhere to secure it by magic and incantations. By contrast, God will send his spirit on all sections of the community so that they mourn for their sins and are then open to miraculous, divine cleansing (Zech. 12.10–13.1). Joel also is much concerned to call the priests to lead the people to lament and fast before Yahweh, and promises that, when they do so, Yahweh will give the gift of rain (2.23-27). In 2.28 (3.1) we also have the promise that God will 'pour out' his spirit 'on all flesh' (the same verb as in Zech. 12.10).

These, then, are some of the parallels with other biblical material which we must take into account when trying to understand what is going on in the book of Joel.

17

THE THEOLOGY AND
FUNCTION OF THE BOOK

THE MOST NATURAL explanation of Joel 1.2–2.27 is that it comprises two separate summonses to penitential fasting and lament in the face of severe natural disasters confronting the community (1.2-20; 2.1-17), with an answering oracle from God (2.18-27). In many ways these are parallel to psalms of communal lament. It has long been recognized that such psalms played a part in the pre-exilic temple ritual. This inference is drawn from the form and structure of such psalms, their general language and, often, their oracular element or, at least, their broken nature in which they switch suddenly to words of praise and thanksgiving (Ps. 22 is an outstanding example of both the general language and the switch in mood); this is reinforced by such a passage as 1 Kings 8. In the act of dedicating the newly built temple Solomon is credited with a prayer in which he envisages the kinds of occasion when the Israelites and their representatives will come into the temple to pray. The vocabulary is so strongly Deuteronomic that it is hard to believe that these were the literal words of Solomon, but that does not affect the fact that such prayer must reflect actual temple practice. Lament is suggested when there has been defeat before enemies (vv. 33-34) or drought (vv. 35-36); and, most interestingly for the book of Joel,

> If there is famine in the land, if there is pestilence or blight or mildew or locust or caterpillar; if their enemy besieges them in any of their cities; whatever plague, whatever sickness there is; whatever prayer, whatever supplication is made by any man or

by all thy people Israel, each knowing the affliction of his own
heart and stretching out his hands toward this house; then hear
thou in heaven thy dwelling place, and forgive and act... (1 Kgs
8.37-39).

There are also other examples in Joel of the form which has
sometimes been called 'prophetic liturgy'.

If parallels to Joel exist which are clearly 'community
laments', it is really useless to try to find a particular event, a
particular disaster or historical context which is reflected in
Joel 1–2. In this connection, R. Simkins is right to see that
Joel's treatment of the catastrophe as identifiable with the
Day of Yahweh was rooted in the concept of myth, and that
his description has many strands drawn from the general
'Day of Yahweh' tradition: the foe from the north, the defeat
of the nations by Yahweh in battle, salvation of the land and
of the people of Yahweh. This, however, makes it all the more
strange that Simkins insists on two particular crises, one a
locust plague in the past and one contemporary, in order to
make his point that Joel brings together both God's cyclical
action as pictured in myth and a linear understanding of how
Yahweh works as he brings his purposes about through
historical events. Surely such material, rooted in the cult and
with many mythical and general overtones, was available for
use at many times of crisis. Nor is there any reason why,
before the exile, a prophet, even a cult prophet, should not
have been sufficiently influenced by prophets like Amos or
Isaiah to invest the distress, whatever it might be, with
ultimate significance by linking the disaster with signs of a
coming Day of Yahweh. In Joel however it is made explicit
(where perhaps with prophets like Amos it was left implicit)
that the disaster can be averted by true repentance and true
observance of the lament ritual. It is true that other examples
of prophets' calling on priests for a torah or some other cultic
direction are found only in post-exilic prophecy (Hag. 2.10-14;
Zech. 7.1-4, with the answer in 8.18-19). But who is to say
that this was not an older tradition—especially since Haggai
links drought, blight and mildew so strongly with the Zion
tradition? According to Haggai all such disasters will be overcome when the temple is rebuilt and Yahweh again reigns

there as universal king. Of course, although we can say that these chapters of Joel are not necessarily pre-exilic, we must also allow that they may be. The lack of any particular historical context excludes certainty. They would not have been out of place in the pre-exilic temple, and they share much of the outlook of pre-exilic prophecy.

It has often been pointed out that in Joel priestly and prophetic interests coincide (see for example Weiser). With Ahlström we can say that Joel believed that a right order in nature and society could only be established by a right use of the Yahweh cult. (We can follow Ahlström in that, while remaining cautious about his belief that Yahweh's promised gift of *hammûreh liṣdāqâh* [2.23], a phrase usually rendered 'early rain for your vindication', was in fact a technical term for a cultic figure, a teacher [*môreh*] or true oracle-giver who, by ordering the cult aright for the people, would secure the gift of rain.) But we should certainly note that correct cultic observance is seen as an expression of a true penitence and a true 'return' to Yahweh (2.12-13). The same kind of care to link cult and proper religious attitudes is found in Haggai, in Zechariah 1–8 and, above all, in Malachi. The answer of Yahweh in Joel 2.18-27 is entirely in terms of 'prophetic eschatology', that is, of God's action in this world's history. There will be renewed fertility, the result of the gift of rain. The 'foe from the north' will be removed, and Yahweh will dwell in the midst of his people protecting them from all future danger. There is really nothing here which cannot be matched in the pre-exilic prophets (for instance Hosea) nor in the Psalms (for instance Pss. 46, 47, 48, 72).

As we have seen, however, such language is capable of re-use and new application at various times. Clearly in the second part of the book of Joel ideas and imagery from the first part are taken up and used again—the very practice which has led so many to assume an inherent unity in the book as the work of one person. But the profound shift in direction evident in 2.28–3.21 (Heb. 3.1–4.21) makes it more likely that this second part comes from other and later circles. Because Joel 1–2 had already linked natural disasters to the 'Day of Yahweh' these circles could take up the same theme.

Because the language describing the disasters was so metaphorical it could serve as a forerunner of later threats, especially as part of that imagery was something as indefinite as the 'foe from the north' tradition. Now, however, the 'Day of Yahweh' is not to be identified with some natural disaster threatening the people of God and so, in this traditional way, a day of darkness. It is now to be seen as the great final gathering of the nations by God for their judgment, and the 'darkness' is that of the cosmic upheavals which will accompany such an act of re-creation of order out of chaos. As such it parallels Isaiah 13, 24–27 and, above all, Zechariah 12–14. There is no call now to repentance and fasting. God will act; and, when he does, this act will reveal those who are truly his, those who 'call on the name of the LORD', and who are thus seen to be those who are called by him. True, the old prophetic promises of fertility and plenty can still be woven into the pattern of hope (3[4].18). To that extent the rain promised in 2.18-27 is seen as 'Heilsregen', rain of salvation, which will be the sign of God's great act of the restoration of nature as well as of people—the sign of cosmic renewal. But the main emphasis now, at this time of threat from the great powers before whom Judah is helpless, is on the turning of the tables: the oppressors will see their own lands devastated while the people of God are protected by Yahweh's presence and renewed by the gift of the divine spirit in a Jerusalem made holy by God's presence (2.28-32 [3.1-5], 3[4].17). It is not merely that Joel sees a transformation from prophetic eschatology towards a more apocalyptic eschatology, but that the cult, with all its metaphor, symbol and roots in the ancient myths, drawing from history and offering the reality of that history afresh in every generation, also points towards the ultimate consummation of history, the final realization of all that is now glimpsed in its repeated rituals only partially and by faith. That is the true nature of the continuing witness of the book of Joel, whose earlier part has furnished hope for people of later and even more desperate times. The enemies the people now face are locusts, drought, fire and invasion, all combined. But the God who has intervened at every time of crisis in their history can be relied upon to intervene again now in a decisive way.

But were such hopes entirely free from partisanship? P.L. Redditt argued that Joel contains a bitter attack on the official Jerusalem priesthood which had allowed the daily sacrifices to fall into abeyance. He notes that Ahlström saw Joel as standing in tension with the Jerusalem cultus because of its impure worship, a view similar to that of Wolff who believed that in reintroducing the theme of 'the Day of Yahweh' Joel was bringing to the fore 'a theme which, if not forgotten, had at least been largely repressed, especially in the leadership circles of Jerusalem'. Redditt believed that Joel and his group represented a prophetic party who had been relegated by the priesthood to the periphery of post-exilic Judaean life. This group then became sectarian, believing that they alone would survive the catastrophe associated with the Day of Yahweh. However, they entertained no hopes of the restoration of a royal figure such as one might expect from a peripheral sector group. Redditt's view is thus quite close to that of Plöger mentioned above.

On the other hand, while we could read the summons to the priests to call a fast and penitential assembly as an attack on them for their 'abdication of leadership' (as Redditt suggests) such an interpretation is not the only possible one. The reason for the cessation of sacrifices is not stated in the text to be the carelessness of the priests or anyone else, but that the locusts, drought and fire had robbed the land of its produce so that there was nothing to offer. Nevertheless, it is here that the many parallels with Zechariah 9–14 become so interesting. In those chapters there certainly are bitter attacks on the 'shepherds' who are seen as false leaders (Zech. 10.1-3; 11.4-14, 15-17; 13.7-9). There also it is stressed that it is only from Yahweh that 'rain' can be effectively sought (10.1-2; 14.17). Also the promise is made there that God will pour out on all sections of the community a 'spirit of compassion and supplication' which will lead them to a true repentance, so that when they look to God 'they shall mourn for him whom they have pierced' (12.10–13.1: the difficulty of the MT has led some English versions to alter the text quite unnecessarily here to read 'when they look on him'. The MT has 'when they look to *me*'. Wellhausen gave perfectly good sense by translating this 'so that they shall look to me. As for him whom they pierced they shall mourn for him'.)

What is the exact force of 2.28-29 (3.1-2) in the book of Joel? In stressing that all sections of the community will receive the spirit of Yahweh so that they will be able to prophesy and have insights normally granted only to a privileged few (cf. Moses' words in Num. 11.29, 'Would that all the LORD's people were prophets and that the LORD would put his spirit upon them'), is this passage really saying that the people will no longer need their religious leaders, priests and prophets? If that were so it would suggest that the circles which took up the first part of the book of Joel and applied it in a new way to their own situation *did* read the calls to the priests there in a hostile and critical way. This would be a very interesting example of early exegesis.

It has often been alleged that apocalyptic is sectarian in origin (cf. Plöger and Hanson). That may well not be true in every case: sometimes a whole community is marginalized by external enemies. Yet the dream that God will overturn the present world orders is one hardly likely to commend itself to the religious or political establishment of any society, especially where these are the same. That such literature is often the literature of the oppressed and the marginalized is well demonstrated by N. Cohn.

The witness of the book of Joel to the hope that ineffective and oppressive leaders may become superfluous because all people, even the humblest, will have a direct experience of God is not good news for the establishment. It probably was not good news for the authorities at Pentecost, when the new Christian church took these words as the charter of its new birth (Acts 2.14-21); and often it has not been welcome in the history of Christendom itself.

In fact, all three prophetic books considered in this volume—Zephaniah, Habakkuk and Joel—testify, like most of the prophetic writings, to a hope that God will establish his right order of 'justice' throughout the kingdoms of this world. This will involve the judgment and defeat of all that distorts or hampers that purpose beyond or within our own societies. Whether such writings come to us as a charter of hope or as a disturbing threat probably depends on which side of the castle gate we have taken up residence.

Further Reading

N. Cohn, *The Pursuit of the Millennium: Revolutionary Millennians and Mystical Anarchists of the Middle Ages* (London: Secker & Warburg, 1957).

P.D. Hanson, *The Dawn of Apocalyptic* (Philadelphia: Fortress Press, 1975).

P.L. Redditt, 'The Book of Joel and Peripheral Prophecy', *CBQ* 48 (1986), pp. 225-40.

R. Simkins, *Yahweh's Activity in History and Nature in the Book of Joel* (Ancient Near Eastern Texts and Studies, 10; Lewiston, NY: Edwin Mellen, 1991).

Weiser, *Das Buch der zwölf kleinen Propheten.*

INDEXES

INDEX OF BIBLICAL REFERENCES

130 Zephaniah, Habbakuk, Joel

INDEX OF AUTHORS